COMBAT ARMS

MODERN

HELICOPTERS

BILL GUNSTON

PRENTICE
HALL
PRESS

NEW YORK • LONDON • TORONTO • SYDNEY • TOKYO • SINGAPORE

A Salamander Book

Prentice Hall Press
15 Columbus Circle
New York, New York 10023

Copyright ©1990 by Salamander Books Ltd.

An Arco Military Book

PRENTICE HALL PRESS and colophons are registered trademarks of Simon & Schuster, Inc.

Originally published in the United Kingdom by Salamander Books Ltd, 129-137 York Way, London N7 9LG.

Library of Congress Catalog Card Number 90-52992.

ISBN 0-13-589847-1

10 9 8 7 6 5 4 3 2 1

First Prentice Hall Press Edition

The Author

Bill Gunston is a former RAF pilot and flying instructor. He has acted as advisor to several aviation companies and has become one of the most internationally respected authors and broadcasters on aviation and scientific subjects. He is author of numerous books on aviation and other military subjects, is a regular contributor to many international defense periodicals, is Assistant Compiler of *Jane's All the World's Aircraft* and was responsible for the companion volume entitled *Modern Fighters*.

Credits

Editor: Richard Collins.
Designer: Rod Ferring.
Color artwork: ©Salamander Books Ltd. and © Pilot Press Ltd.
Filmset by The Old Mill, London.
Color reproduction: Track Origination.
Printed in Belgium by: Proost International Book Production, Turnhout.

Contents

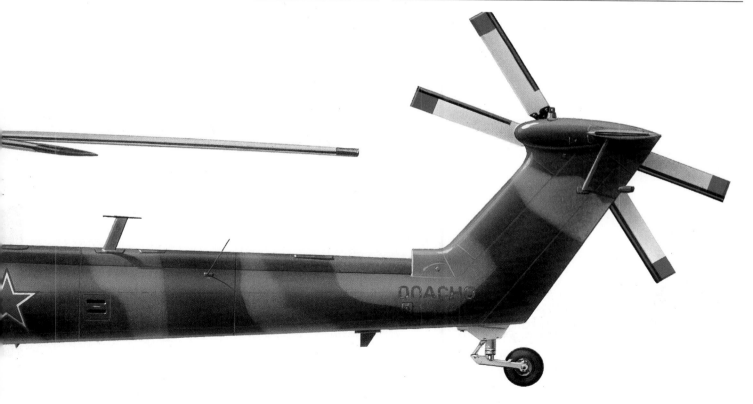

EARLY THIS century Henry Ford said, in so many words, "The airplane won't amount to a damn until it can go straight up and down, and hover." In this he was wide of the mark, but the fact still remains that the ability to go straight up and down, and hover, is often extremely important. It has resulted in today's helicopter market running at the rate of several billion pounds or dollars per year.

Apart from that ability the helicopter has little to offer. Compared with an aeroplane of similar installed power the helicopter carries much less, flies slower, has a much shorter range, gives its occupants a ride the noise and vibration of which would never be accepted from a fixed-wing machine, and generally incurs much higher costs. One might think the ability to hover would make the helicopter particularly safe, but the reverse is true, as seen in the tremendous contrast between aeroplane and helicopter insurance premiums. And most pilots would agree that helicopters are much more difficult to fly than most equivalent aeroplanes.

This book is concerned specifically with helicopters that can be described as "combat arms". Included under this heading are machines designed solely for transport, but helicopters — probably more even than aeroplanes — can operate right in the front line in the face of the enemy. This certainly qualifies even relatively simple transport helicopters as "combat arms". Most of the helicopters in this book, however, are equipped with very comprehensive avionics and other devices to enable them to fly some kind of "fighting" mission. Indeed, one helicopter now flying, said to be the Soviet Ka-41, is the nearest thing we have yet seen to a helicopter fighter, tasked primarily with shooting down hostile aircraft.

Such a machine clearly needs all the speed and agility possible, and it is strange that the Ka-41 appears to have traditional co-axial rotors which impose a severe limit on speed. In the USA a co-axial helicopter has flown in a shallow dive at over 300mph (482km/h), but it had special rotors. This is one of several possibilities discussed in the first section below. Other subjects covered include airframes, propulsion, sensors, weapons and cockpits.

Above: Forerunner of today's V-22 Osprey, the Bell XV-15 tilt-rotor research vehicle has been used to provide test data relating to the principles of tilt-rotor flight. Power is provided by a pair of wingtip-mounted turboshaft engines, here being raised to the vertical.

Performance

Thanks to its advanced BERP (British experimental rotor programme) main rotor, an otherwise almost standard Westland Lynx has pushed up the world helicopter speed record to a remarkable 249mph (401km/h). The author can remember when that was faster than any fighter in the RAF. But this is very much the exception. Most helicopters cannot be pushed much beyond 150mph (242km/h), and the most numerous aircraft anywhere in the Western world (since 1945), the familiar "Huey", has a "never exceed speed" of only 127mph (204km/h). It is therefore hardly surprising that great efforts have been made to try to find ways to make helicopters go faster, or alternatively to develop some other kind of aircraft that can do all a helicopter can do and still fly at much higher speed.

We must not overlook the progress already made with conventional helicopters. Only 30 years ago plenty of helicopters, such as the Bell 47 and S-55, cruised at 85mph (137km/h), or one-third of the Lynx's speed. But in the author's opinion we are unlikely to do very much better without some kind of major "breakthrough". So far all the promising schemes have come to nothing, except for the ABC and the tilt-rotor, and some purists would say the latter is not a helicopter at all.

To deal with the tilt-rotor first, we omitted it from this book because it is really an aeroplane whose very large propellers can be vectored to blow to the rear, for high-speed flight, or downwards, for powered lift. In cruising flight the tilt-rotor is in all respects an aeroplane, with an aeroplane-type tail and lifted by a wing with ailerons or spoilers. Bell built experimental versions in 1954, but nothing more happened until 1977 when the first Bell XV-15 began flying. This quite small research machine led to today's V-22 Osprey, developed by Bell and Boeing in partnership. With two 6,150shp Allison engines, driving 38ft (11.58m) propellers (or they could be called rotors), the V-22 can take off vertically at 47,500lb (21,545kg) and with a short run at 55,000lb (24,947kg). It has a cabin with a cross-section 6ft (1.83m) square, big enough for 24 combat-equipped troops and two gunners, or 12 stretchers and medical attendants or ten tons of cargo. But the big

advantage of the tilt-rotor is that it is not constrained by the aerodynamic and propulsion limits of the helicopter, and it can cruise at 345mph (556km/h).

Obviously this means you get there quicker, but it has another massive advantage. Compared with a helicopter burning fuel at the same rate you travel roughly three times further for each gallon or kilogramme of fuel. In other words the tilt-rotor has about three times the range or radius of action. Understandably, all the US armed forces showed a great interest in such a capable vehicle, especially for such missions as long-range assault, SAR (search and rescue), ASW (anti-submarine warfare) and special forces operations. Yet since 1988 there have been obvious political moves in the United States to kill off the V-22 Osprey entirely. It has been repeatedly deleted from the Defense Budget and, rather like the Harrier and AV-8B, only restored after prolonged and frantic lobbying by the Marines, who are the most urgent customers.

The ridiculous stance taken on Capitol Hill is that the V-22 is not needed because the missions can be flown by helicopters. Nobody has yet suggested which helicopter could fly the missions. For example, the US Navy combat search and rescue mission calls for a 530 mile (852km) outward journey, a 15min hover (under severe conditions), the rescue of four survivors and then a 530 mile return, all in 3hr 45min. No helicopter could come anywhere near this performance.

Why the attitude of the US Department of Defense, or their political advisors, to the V-22 is so strange is that it seems

Above: Much larger than the XV-15, the Bell/Boeing V-22 Osprey has much to offer, but is likely to fall victim to drastic defence budget cuts.

obvious that tilt-rotors must in the fairly short term take about half the total helicopter market. The point was made earlier that helicopters have succeeded commercially solely because their ability to hover, and to land on small back-lawns and constricted decks is so useful that it outweighs their other disadvantages. Now it can be shown that, the lower the velocity of the "jet" produced by the lifting system, then, in general, the less the noise and the higher the efficiency in hovering flight. Jet-lift aircraft, such as the Harrier, have a high jet velocity, so they are noisy and inefficient in hovering flight. Thus, nobody would buy one if the mission called for extended hovering. Jet-lift aircraft are bought for their high-speed performance, and they spend as little time hovering as possible. In contrast, the helicopter is efficient in hovering flight,

Osprey Performance

Right: In terms of its overall performance capabilities in the operational flight envelope, the Osprey is far superior to the US Marine Corps' principle medium-lift helicopter, the CH-46E Sea Knight. This aircraft-like performance, combined with its troop and cargo carrying capacity, is obviously a strong selling point; but will it be enough to save the project?

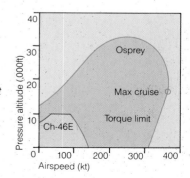

Left: Very much an idea for the future, but one which could easily come to fruition, is Sikorsky's stopped-rotor concept. The four-bladed Circulation-controlled Rotor (CCR) has all its blades angled at 45° when not in use, resulting in the vehicle attaining performance similar to that of an aircraft. The power from the engines then takes over to boost maximum attainable speed to approximately Mach 0.8.

Below: Invented in Great Britain, but developed and tested in the United States, the CCR concept has been tested on board an HH-2D. Note how the thin sheet of air is blown downwards over the trailing-edge of each blade to enhance overall lift.

because it has the lowest "jet" velocity of all, but it suffers in cruising flight (see Propulsion section below). Thus, helicopters will continue to be bought wherever the mission demands extended hovering. If we were certain the survivor to be rescued, or the submarine to be detected and sunk, was never going to be very far away, then the mission is one for a helicopter because it involves protracted hovering.

But most missions are not like this. They often require no hovering at all, merely a takeoff from one small patch of ground or deck and a landing on another. The hovering part of the flight might be seconds only, and the hovering at each end might be many hundreds of miles apart. This is obviously a mission for the tilt-rotor. Indeed, virtually all the thousands of executive helicopters in the world could with advantage be replaced by tilt-rotors (if they existed), because their mission is to fly from A to B as fast as possible, without protracted hovering. Yet the determination of the Bush Administration to kill the Osprey merely makes it harder for US industry to cash in on this gigantic market, which just could go elsewhere. A later edition of this book written in year 2000 could well see half the helicopters replaced by tilt-rotors.

There have been many other attempts to overcome the helicopters's performance limitations, but most have fallen by the wayside. One of the most promising was begun in Britain in 1963 as the CCR (circulation-controlled rotor). If compressed air is blown at high velocity from narrow slits along particular parts of the edges of the rotor blades it is possible to make the blade lift even if it has a completely symmetric profile, like a flat oval. The idea was that the helicopter should have auxiliary propulsion, such as jet engines, which could accelerate to high speed while the drive to the rotor was allowed to run down and finally stop. Because of its symmetric profile the blade could be made to behave like a wing no matter

The Circulation-controlled Rotor

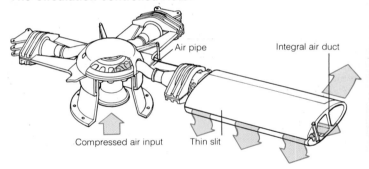

Air pipe

Integral air duct

Compressed air input

Thin slit

whether the air was blowing across it from leading edge to trailing edge (as on one side of the helicopter) or in the reverse direction (as on the other side). In the USA the idea was called the X-wing, or "stopped rotor", and it was tested by NASA on the Sikorsky S-72. Suffice to say there were problems.

Another promising idea was the ABC (advancing blade concept). Here the helicopter was to be lifted by co-axial rotors, mounted close together and each fitted with exceptionally rigid blades mounted firmly in the hub without any of the usual flapping hinges. Thus, no matter what loads might be encountered, the blades could not collide with each other. There was nothing terribly complex about the idea, which promised to overcome the basic difficulty that stands in the way of a fast helicopter. This difficulty is that, as forward speed increases, so does the helicopter's own speed become greater than the airspeed of the blade due to its own rotation. This does not bother the advancing half of the rotor, where the blades are coming round head-on to the air. Here we merely have to reduce the pitch of the blades to maintain constant lift. The problem occurs on the other half of the rotor,

Right: In contrast to conventional (top) and co-axial (middle) main rotor configurations, the Advanced Blade Concept (ABC) helicopter has a quite different rotor arrangement (bottom). The co-axial configuration is utilised again, but this time the pairs of blades are set much closer together. This arrangement results in an equal amount of lift being produced on either side of the helicopter during flight.

Below: So far, the Sikorsky S-69 (military designation: XH-59A) is the only ABC-configured helicopter to have flight-tested this blade concept in details. Lift generated actually increases up to speeds of approximately 300mph (482km/h).

The ABC Helicopter

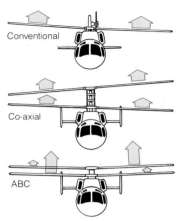

Conventional

Co-axial

ABC

been done to take this promising idea further. It is equally surprising that the Kamov Ka-41, which is credited by NATO analysts with a speed of 217mph (350km/h) in battle trim, should retain the traditional articulated type of co-axial rotors.

Today the only proven way of making faster helicopters — apart from the obvious answers of more engine power, lighter weight or less drag — is to use improved blades on the main rotor. The current world helicopter speed record is held by a Westland Lynx with BERP blades (British experimental rotor programme). These have thin sweptback tips, an aft-loaded outer section (most of the lift is generated further back from the leading edge than normal) and a reflexed inner section where downwash is reduced. One may expect to see such blades introduced progressively to production helicopters, beginning with 12 Super Lynx ordered by South Korea for use by its navy.

Airframes

The first helicopters were often ungainly in appearance. Aerodynamic drag was not of great importance, because their speed was similar to that of aeroplanes of the pre-1914 era, namely about 65-75mph (100-120km/h). Today nearly all helicopters can fly at about twice this speed, and streamlining is important. Unfortunately, especially in the case of "combat helicopters", avionics and other mission equipment make the final result look cluttered. One Soviet helicopter has its streamlined shape marred by 38 different bulges, bumps, boxes, rods and similar devices which all have to be stuck on the outside!

where the so-called "retreating" blades are moving backwards.

At quite a low speed the inboard part of each retreating blade will experience air flowing in the reverse direction, from trailing edge to leading edge. This area will rapidly get larger as the forward speed of the helicopter increases. Before long there will be only a quite small area at the tip of the blade where lift is being generated. The blade angle will then have reached the stalling point. Any further increase in the helicopter's speed will result in the retreating blades stalling. The helicopter will then receive no lift from the retreating blades, and it will not only drop like a stone but will also roll over. It is retreating blade stall that stops us from having a production helicopter that can fly at 200mph (322km/h). But if we use rigid co-axial blades we can forget about the lift from the retreating blades, because we now have advancing blades on both sides of the helicopter. The Sikorsky S-69, in a programme funded mainly by the US Army, flew successfully at 316mph (509km/h). No insuperable problems were encountered, and it appears surprising that nothing has

More than half the world total of helicopters have airframes of what might be termed the pod-and-boom type. We could build aeroplanes the same way, with a fat but quite short fuselage to house everything and a long narrow tube to carry the tail. With helicopters different designers adopt different solutions. To take Sikorsky as an example, the S-55 (British Whirlwind) was very much a pod-and-boom machine, the S-58 (Wessex) switched to having a full-length fuselage and the S-61 (Sea King) introduced the amphibious boat hull. It goes without saying that the switch from piston to turbine engines greatly facilitated the introduction of improved airframes, because the lighter and more compact powerplants can be mounted on top as close as possible to the main-rotor gearbox. Moreover, today's engines need no complex and drag-producing cooling system, though every helicopter still has to have some kind of heat exchanger to cool the lubricating oil for the main gearbox. Combat helicopters are as far as possible designed so that they can continue flying usually for 30 minutes, after they have suffered battle damage causing total loss of oil.

Combat helicopters likely to suffer battle damage also need to do their best to survive in the face of enemy fire. As every foot-soldier today can be armed with a shoulder-fired SAM (surface-to-air missile) it may seem pointless to design a helicopter merely to survive being hit by a bullet, but the philosophy is that this is much better than nothing, and the ability to resist fire from modest-calibre automatic weapons does give a helicopter a much better chance of getting back to its base. The common objective is for the whole helicopter (if possible) to resist strikes by 0.5in (12.7mm) bullets (which can include high-explosive or armour-piercing rounds), and for the special class of armed anti-armour helicopters to do their best to withstand hits by 23mm shells. Curiously, many combat helicopters claim to resist cannon fire yet seat the crew behind a thin plastic canopy that would not stop a 0.22 round!

The universal trend away from metal rotor blades and towards composite blades has probably improved ability to survive battle damage, though many composite blades still retain metal spars which, if severed, would result in loss of the helicopter. A few, such as the Apache, have multiple spars which have proved to be highly resistant to 23mm strikes. Clearly, it helps if multiple redundant load paths can be provided, so that nothing catastrophic happens even if one part is shot through. The main transmission, however, cannot be duplicated. In the Apache crucial parts of the transmission are protected by being surrounded by collars of ESR (electro-slag refined) steel. The Apache's crew are also protected against fire from below by lightweight boron carbide armour. As for systems, the Apache has two completely separate hydraulically powered controls for both rotors, and if both should be knocked out (and in theory this can never be ac-complished by a single hit) then the flight-controls automatically revert to secondary fly by wire.

The Apache is thus representative of the most survivable type of design of the 1978-80 period. Helicopters designed since then have tended to have ever-greater proportions of composites in their construction. Such materials as carbon (graphite) fibre, glassfibre, Kevlar (a fibre akin to spider web) and Nomex (a family of Nylon/phenolic honeycombs) are all important, usually bonded by some type of epoxy resin. Such materials are tremendously strong in relation to their weight, and it could be claimed that they stand up better than metal to battle damage. Their only real fault is that they are generally softer than metal and so do not stand up so well to prolonged abrasion or high-velocity impact with rain and hail. The leading edge of a composite rotor blade is therefore protected by an anti-abrasion strip of steel, nickel or titanium.

It is convenient here to glance at a few current projects, partly to see what they are made of and partly in order to include helicopters which otherwise would have to be omitted from the book because they do not yet exist. For example, while the Italian Agusta company used ordinary aluminium alloy to build the A 109 and A 129, the A 129 developments are being studied with up to 70 per cent composite construction. The Tonal anti-tank helicopter (if JEH, Joint European Helicopters, comprising firms in Britain, Italy, the Netherlands and Spain are ever allowed to go ahead) would be mainly composite, while the LBH (Light Battlefield Helicopter), a 12-seat support version, which might be built by Agusta with partners in Argentina and Australia, would probably be metal/composites about 50/50. The Eurocopter Tiger, featured in this book, would be virtually 100 per cent composites. The NH 90, being developed by companies in

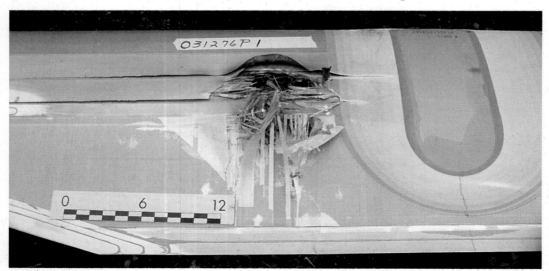

Left: Proof of the inherent strength of modern main rotor blades can be seen to good effect in this AH-64A Apache blade. Despite having its interior and exterior badly damaged, by a cannon shell, the blade managed to fly on for another five hours.

Right: With a potential requirement for over 2,000 production examples, aerospace industry interest in the US Army's Light Helicopter (LH) programme is obviously keen. A wide range of possible configurations have appeared in various artistic impressions; this example being a product of the partnership between Bell and McDonnell Douglas, which is one of the partnerships now in contention for design selection.

Above: A multi-national helicopter project, the NH90 (NATO Helicopter for the '90s) is to be procured in two major versions: navalized ASW and tactical troop transport. The latter is illustrated here.

OH-58 and AH-1 were designed, and that with proper planning and funding a further revolution can take place on the drawing board, so that when an LH helicopter is actually built, some time in the 1990s, it will be of a design that will remain competitive until at least 2030.

The requirement for the LH has varied over the years, and early in the programme was expected to exceed a total of 5,000. As this book is written, in 1990, the planned total is 2,096, in three variants: armed reconnaissance, light attack and (a new mission outside the Soviet Union) air-to-air combat. The competing firms have organized themselves into two powerful teams: Bell Helicopter and McDonnell Douglas and Boeing Helicopters and Sikorsky. Each team is supported by a carefully picked back-up team of specialist companies, mainly in the sphere of avionics. So important is the LH programme that the competitors have spent large sums of their own money in undertaking preliminary research programmes. At present they are working on a 23-month demonstration and validation phase, which is expected to lead to a choice of a single basic LH design in 1991-2.

One of Bell's early studies was for a small and agile tilt-rotor aircraft. The Army then announced that it required a helicopter of conventional type, which may well be justified if the various missions all demand prolonged hovering. Accordingly all LH studies have since 1989 been narrowed down to small and streamlined helicopters, each powered by two 1,200shp LHTEC (Allison and Garrett in partnership) T800 engines driving advanced main rotors with four blades (looking like the BERP) held in bearingless hubs, and with totally composite materials throughout, except for points of exceptionally high stress where steel, titanium or light alloy is inescapable.

West Germany, France, Italy and the Netherlands, and likely to go into full development before this book appears, will have composite blades and "a high level of composites" in the fuselage. The P 120L, a 2.3 tonne (5,071lb) helicopter being developed by companies in France, China and Singapore, will have a composites fraction exceeding 80 per cent. The partners on the P 120L estimate the market at 1,500 to 2,000 units, showing how the building of helicopters, 20 years ago the prerogative of five countries, is now a worldwide activity.

Airframe structural design has been a major consideration in the world's biggest current helicopter research programme, for the planned US Army LH (Light Helicopter). This programme was launched in 1982, but it is not a slick requirement that can quickly be met. Rather has it arisen from the recognition that the entire technology of the helicopter has already been revolutionized since such machines as the UH-1,

11

Propulsion

The point has already been made that, in the mid-1950s, the replacement of piston engines by gas turbines absolutely revolutionized the helicopter and made such machines far more attractive. Today a few of the very smallest and lightest helicopters still have piston engines, but every combat helicopter capable of flying a military or naval mission is powered by one or more gas turbines. These can burn a range of fuels, normally some form of jet fuel of kerosene type but often including MT (motor transport) gasolines commonly used by armies or diesel oil as used by both armies and navies.

Most helicopter engines are of the free-turbine type. One turbine drives the compressor, and a completely independent LP (low-pressure) turbine further downstream is connected by a shaft which can emerge at either end of the engine to drive the main gearbox of the helicopter. The main part of a free-turbine engine can be started independently of the power turbine, though of course as the gas flow through the power turbine builds up it will experience a torque and want to rotate. Normally a clutch is inserted between the engine and the helicopter main gearbox. This enables either part to rotate independently. For example, either engine of a twin-engined helicopter can fly the machine with the other engine shut down.

The engines drive what are called the helicopter's dynamic parts. These comprise the transmission, a series of tubular drive shafts which spin at high speed, held in low-friction bearings and connected by various joints or angle boxes which allow for any desired change in direction between one shaft and the next. For example there will be an angle box where the tail boom meets the fin (tail rotor pylon) to turn the drive through something like 70°. Altogether the transmission may look quite complicated, with a drive from a primary gearbox on each engine direct to the main gearbox and then secondary shafts driving the tail rotor and, often, a big fan to draw air through the oil-cooling radiator. In a combat helicopter the entire transmission must be designed to survive battle damage.

Since the mid-1950s gas turbines have been constantly improved. For any given power output they have become smaller, lighter and yet tougher and better able to resist birdstrikes and bullets. Paradoxically, a major factor in this process has been replacement of axial compressors by the centrifugal type, which 35 years ago was thought almost obsolete! To show the extent of the improvement wrought by the engine designers, in 1955 the Alouette II, a pioneer turbine-engined helicopter, was powered by the Turbomeca Artouste II which weighed 261lb (118kg) and at the maximum continuous output of 320shp burned 352lb/h of fuel. Today the T800 engine

The LHTEC T800 Engine

Above: Just as the design for the LH has yet to be finalised, so the choice of powerplant remains open to contenders. Illustrated is one of the competing designs, namely the Light Helicopter Turbine Engine Company (LHTEC) 1,200shp high-efficiency T800 engine.

planned for the LH and many other helicopters weighs about 292lb, it is rated at 1,200shp and burns 530lb/h of fuel. In other words, fuel consumption has gone up by just fifty per cent but power has gone up (for an engine of similar size) by *four times*!

In 1946 Cierva used the sideways thrust of a jet of pumped air in the W.9 helicopter to counteract the torque of the main rotor. This meant the tail rotor could be eliminated. The W.9 was completely successful, but nothing more was done until McDonnell Douglas flew their first NOTAR (NO Tail Rotor) helicopter in 1981. This expels pumped air along a narrow slit along the tail boom in such a way that the airflow induced around the boom gives a side thrust proportional to engine power and rotor torque. A further air exit is in the end of the boom with control shutters connected to the pilot's pedals for directional control. McDonnell Douglas claim the NOTAR reduced operating costs, reduced pilot workload, enhanced safety and improved flight characteristics, especially when travelling to the side or rear. Absence of a tail rotor should also reduce the helicopter's noise and radar signatures. The first combat helicopter with NOTAR is the McDonnell Douglas 520N Black Tiger. There may in due course be military and naval versions of the MDX, designed as a NOTAR helicopter from the outset.

Every combat helicopter in future will have to be a stealth, or "low observables", type aircraft. No helicopter in close system is bulky, complex, heavy and quite expensive, all with the objective of leaving nothing that could form a target for a heat-seeking missile.

This is in sharp contrast to modern fixed-wing combat aircraft whose jetpipes broadcast heat at perhaps 12 to 40 times the rate of battlefield helicopters, yet whose IR signature is almost ignored. Doubtless the answer is simply that it is too difficult to tone down or obscure the thermal radiation of an afterburner nozzle, whereas with a helicopter the IR signature can be reduced near to zero.

Defensive systems

Continuing with the same argument, the modern helicopter has an urgent need for similar defensive equipment to that fitted to fast jets. By defensive systems one could include weapons and armour, but these are dealt with elsewhere. The normal meaning of the term is equipment of an avionic nature designed to protect the helicopter against hostile radars, heat-homing missiles and similar dangers. At once, we again find that, while plenty has been done at IR wavelengths, few helicopters have much protection at the longer wavelengths of radar or the shorter wavelengths of lasers.

So far as is known, no helicopter yet flying has an airframe incorporating ''stealth'' features to reduce RCS (radar cross section). There is not the slightest doubt that whatever helicopter wins the LH competition will have been designed with this need in mind, but it is still likely to have a large and distinctive radar signature. Most current helicopters, because of their rotor-system geometry and rotational speed, can even be positively identified by type at a range of up to 30 miles (48km), though, of course, the radar has to be able to see them. Little has been published on methods of making helicopters, and especially their rotors, invisible to hostile radars. With a large fuselage or wing it is possible to achieve reductions in RCS of perhaps 99.9 per cent by suitable shaping and the use of RAM (radar absorbent materials), but these techniques are much more difficult with rotor blades.

Several modern missiles are laser guided, using various techniques. Those that fly along a laser beam aimed at the helicopter by a human operator are clearly immune to countermeasures at laser wavelengths. All one can do against such missiles is to make the helicopter difficult to see. In the past 30 years the science of camouflage and low-observability painting has made important progress, but every helicopter in this book could still be instantly detected by eye and destroyed by a SAM of this nature.

Only in the single case of IR-homing missiles has much been done to protect the helicopter. The reduction of IR signature near to zero has already been reported. Many helicopters also have the ability to eject a succession of flares

Above: A recent and revolutionary aspect of helicopter design is the No Tail Rotor (NOTAR) design, seen here on the McDonnel Douglas OH-6A *test-bed. Developed on behalf of the US Army, this concept is to be applied to civilian helicopters as well as their military counterparts.*

NOTAR Technology

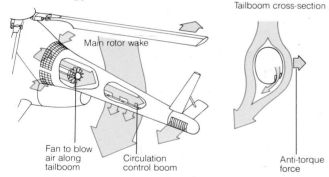

Tailboom cross-section

Main rotor wake

Fan to blow air along tailboom

Circulation control boom

Anti-torque force

Above: Compressed air is blown from a slit along the tailboom, with the *airflow around the boom generating the necessary amount of side thrust.*

proximity to the enemy can expect to approach, attack and escape at such a high speed that the defences cannot react in time. Most of today's helicopters can be heard coming for minutes before they can be seen, so there would be little point in trying to reduce their radar cross-section. Since 1980 there has been a revolution in the IR signature of most battlefield and naval helicopters. Their hot jetpipes have been shrouded behind cool enclosures, and turned upwards (sometimes, as in the Mi-28, downwards) to direct their hot efflux away where it cannot trigger IR-sensitive detectors. In such front-line machines as the Apache and Mi-28 the engine exhaust and/or to switch on an active IRCM device. The latter is like a lighthouse that pumps out IR radiation in all directions, but with the emissions pulsed or coded by a precisely timed sub-system. The resulting on/off radiation confuses enemy heat-seeking missiles, causing them to break lock and fall harmlessly away. Flares are pyrotechnics like fireworks which, ignited as they are shot out of the aircraft, burn with a bright flame to give an IR source far more attractive than the helicopter, thus decoying enemy missiles away. What has yet to be explained is whether any useful purpose can be served by IRCM jammers and flares if we have already virtually eliminated our helicopter's IR signature.

Almost every combat helicopter today is equipped with an avionics system which in Britain often goes under the loose title of ESM, meaning "electronic support (or surveillance) measures". In other countries each installation is given a more explicit title, such as an RWR (radar warning receiver) or IRWS (infra-red warning system). Other such devices work at laser wavelengths. All of them are passive; in other words, they do not emit, but are extremely sensitive to incoming signals or radiation aimed at the helicopter.

In a very few cases the helicopter's mission is such that it can safely be concluded that all hostile activity will be confined to an area ahead of the helicopter's nose. Usually, however, with the machine darting and turning in different directions, enemy anti-helicopter systems could be active in any direction, so the defensive systems have to give all-round cover. Some of the most prominent ESM systems are seen on naval helicopters. Royal Navy Lynx helicopters carry Racal MIR-2 (code name Orange Crop) in boxes above the nose and on the rear fuselage, while the SH-60B Seahawk has the surprisingly obtrusive Raytheon ALQ-142, with four square receiver antennas (two on the nose and two where the fuselage tapers sharply in plan) each covering a 90° sector.

Left: Although representative of an earlier generation of battlefield anti-tank helicopters, the Bell AH-1 is nevertheless a highly capable weapons platform. Though it does not have a roof- or mast-mounted sight, the undernose gun's direction of fire can be controlled by helmet sights worn by the pilot and/or co-pilot, or by use of the M65 TOW missile system's telescopic sight unit. A comprehensive package of defensive avionics is also fitted for self-protection.

Above: Carrying a BAe Sea Eagle anti-ship missile on its port side, this Royal Navy Westland Sea King HAS.5 is an updated model used in the ASW role. A variety of sensors are carried to enable the crew to carry out their mission, the most obvious of which is the MEL Super Searcher radar housed in the large dorsal radome aft of the main cabin. Note the Racal MIR-2 Orange Crop ESM receiver boxes on the nose, each of which has a wide area of coverage.

Almost certainly the most numerous RWR in service on 11 types of Western helicopter (and many fixed-wing machines) is the E-Systems APR-39, which normally needs two pairs of unobtrusive spiral antennas, each looking like a flat disc about 8in (20cm) in diameter, and a single small blade antenna about the size of a hand. This covers a wide range of radar bands (different frequencies) and not only warns the crew but can determine the frequency, PRF (pulse-repetition frequency), pulse width, persistence and threshold power of the hostile radar, and also display the direction of the threat on a cockpit indicator. Future helicopters will use such systems to give automatic control of anti-radar defensive systems, such as chaff dispensers and active jammers. Not many helicopters carry active jammers, but the ITT ALQ-136 is standard aboard the US Army AH-64A Apache, and the Whittaker ALQ-167 (British code name Yellow Veil) pod was installed on Royal Navy Lynx HAS.3s patrolling the Persian (Arabian) Gulf in 1987.

There is just one reservation about all these avionic goodies. While helicopters are noisy and obtrusive from a distance of several miles it matters little, because their presence will be obvious (except when every enemy soldier or sailor is enclosed in his own noisy vehicle or ship). But when helicopters start being stealthy and hard to detect the last thing they wish to do is start broadcasting their presence by firing off a pyrotechnic display of chaff and flares and sending out high-power radar or IR jamming radiation, all triggered automatically (perhaps to the great surprise of the crew) by a supposedly protective ESM system.

Sensors

It is already obvious that for a modern helicopter to fly its mission it relies totally upon avionics. It needs avionics partly to navigate, partly to find targets (or avoid enemies), partly to communicate with friendly forces and partly to defend itself. We are concerned here chiefly with devices which enable the helicopter to navigate accurately, fly safely in close proximity to the ground, detect targets and aim weapons. The equipment fit is also intimately related to the design of the cockpit(s), and even with the helmets worn by the crew. Gradually a perfect overall system for an attack helicopter is being evolved. In 1990 we might be about half-way towards this objective.

Some 30 years ago, in the early 1960s, few helicopters even carried radar, and this was usually for overwater use. NOE (nap of the Earth) flying had to be done entirely by hand, the pilot looking ahead visually. Hundreds of helicopters practised this, and not a few came to grief through hitting unseen obstructions, the most frequent impacts being with power lines and other kinds of wire or cable. Such casualties con-

tinued even after tactical helicopters had begun to be equipped with radar or FLIR (forward-looking infra-red) or even magnifying optical sights.

The latter were the first type of sensor to be fitted in large numbers. Their need was highlighted by France's development of the wire-guided anti-tank missile, the first versions of which were the SS.10 and SS.11. Such missiles can have an effective range up to 2.5 miles (4km), and in order to steer them so that they hit their tank targets the operator needed a special kind of sighting system. This was usually mounted in the cockpit roof, and gyrostabilised so that it stayed pointing in any desired direction irrespective of the pitching, rolling, yawing and vibration that characterized all early helicopters. The sight was basically a combination of a periscope and a telescope, the latter having two magnifications (typically x 2 and x 10). The big magnification was useful for finding targets, but its field of view was so restricted

Below: The Ferranti AF500 roof-mounted sight is just one of several such pieces of equipment now fitted to a variety of battlefield combat helicopters. Key features include a gyro-stabilised head and a cockpit down-tube, this latter item being adjustable for height. The head can be steered through 240° azimuth, and the whole unit can be operated in conjunction with a laser designator and rangefinder unit.

A Roof-mounted Sight

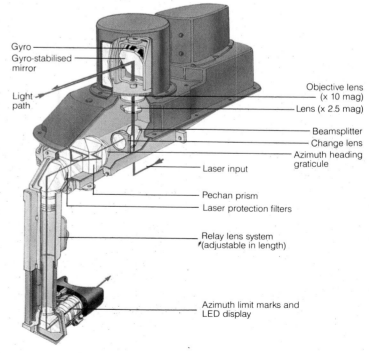

Gyro
Gyro-stabilised mirror
Light path
Objective lens (x 10 mag)
Lens (x 2.5 mag)
Beamsplitter
Change lens
Azimuth heading graticule
Laser input
Pechan prism
Laser protection filters
Relay lens system (adjustable in length)
Azimuth limit marks and LED display

that the low magnification was needed to capture or gather the missile. When the missile was known to be on the direct line to the target the operator could switch to high power and use this to guide the missile on to the target.

Anti-tank helicopters still need an optical sight of this kind, and the obvious place to install the actual optical head, or objective lens, is on a mast high above the main rotor. Like an infantryman looking through a periscope from a protective trench, the MMS (mast-mounted sight) enables the vulnerable helicopter to stay out of sight while it watches enemy armour and picks out targets. The sight head is carried on a rigid tube passing through a hole in the centre of the main rotor hub, the optical path subsequently being determined by lenses and prisms which convey the image to the eyepiece in the cockpit. Switching from one magnification to another is done by various instant-reacting methods. At full magnification the field of view is very small — only a degree or two — and vibration or angular movement of the helicopter has a much greater effect on the viewed scene, so the pointing accuracy in this mode has to be of a very high standard indeed.

Ordinary optics naturally cannot be used to see through bad weather, or under any conditions at night. For bad weather a longer wavelength is necessary, such as radar or an FLIR. Radar has the best penetration through rain, smoke or other obscuration, but the picture definition tends to be poor (so that, for example, it would be difficult to spot a tank against a hillside at 4km). The FLIR gives much better picture definition, and also has the enormous advantage that it is a passive (non-emitting) system. Radar sends out waves or signals which can be detected by the enemy, warning of the presence of the helicopter even before it could be heard, or detected by the enemy's own radar. There is no way the enemy can be aware that a helicopter's FLIR is quietly presenting high-definition pictures of all that he is doing, even on the darkest night. So far FLIRs have not been used as the sole aid in detecting targets and guiding missiles to strike them, but this ought to be possible. Of course, the next generation of missiles will include some that are self-homing (see Weapons section).

Some FLIR sensors have been used to warn of wires and other obstructions, but there are many experts who consider the only reliable way of detecting such hazards is to use a radar operating on millimetric wavelengths. Ordinary (centimetric) radars would be unlikely to detect the wire. An MMW (millimetric wave) radar can be made very compact, often the whole package fitting into a nose thimble similar to that which in other radars houses just the antenna. The waves are short enough to be reflected by the wire, or to give good definition against other targets. An MMW radar also appears to be an excellent TFR (terrain-following radar), to guide the

Above: The HOT missiles carried in the side-mounted pod will be guided to their target(s) in poor weather by the Venus Ball FLIR nose turret.

Right: The optics within this set of Cat's Eyes Night Vision Goggles (NVGs) are set above the wearer's line of sight.

helicopter automatically along undulating ground whilst maintaining a chosen altitude, such as 5ft (1.5m). Some helicopters even need a radar so that, in bad weather, they can rendezvous with a tanker to take on fuel, via a probe which can be extended to ensure that the hose never comes near the main rotor.

Key to McDonnell Douglas mast-mounted sight
1 Laser rangefinder/designator
2 Stabilised platform
3 TV camera
4 Boresight assembly
5 Thermal imaging sensor
6 Multiplexer electronics
7 Composite post
8 Heat exchanger

Mast-mounted Sight

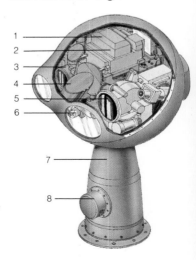

Right: While some combat helicopters sport roof-mounted sights, others rely on the use of mast-mounted sights, such as this model produced by McDonnell Douglas for use on the Bell OH-85D in service with the US Army. The sight can be used for day and night viewing, and houses an auto-focusing (IR) thermal imaging sensor, 12x magnification TV camera, laser rangefinder/designator and an automatic boresighting and target tracking in flight facility.

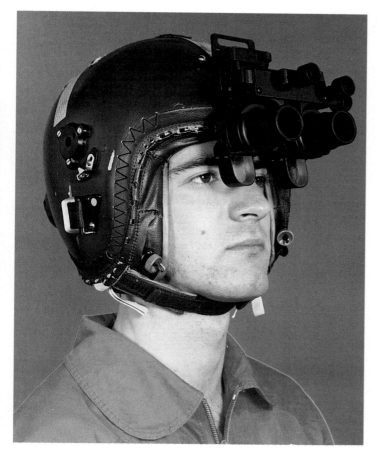

night. Electronic methods multiply this stream by thousands of times so that, when the enhanced flow hits a sensitive surface (rather like a TV screen) a visible picture results even on a dark night. NVGs have to be light and not cumbersome, and one of the bigger technical problems has been designing NVGs through which the wearer can clearly see the cockpit controls and instruments. NVGs are not the same as an HMD (helmet-mounted display), in which a tiny cathode-ray tube or similar avionic device presents the wearer with vital information focused on a transparent screen in front of his eyes (or in front of one eye). The real challenge is to combine all the separate wavelengths, and separate devices, into a single combined system.

Nobody quite knows how to do this. Many research teams have come to the conclusion that, as tomorrow's helicopter crews are going to have to rely so heavily on avionics anyway, the normal cockpit transparencies should be dispensed with. Instead the crew would wear helmets incorporating combined night vision devices and the displays from various sensors, operating at different wavelengths. The sensors would be aimed automatically by one of the crew moving his head. The effect would be as if, instead of human eyes, the pilot or CPG (co-pilot/gunner) had a radar, FLIR, laser and possibly other sensors built into his head. His external vision would be approximately the same no matter whether it was day or night, or a clear day or thick fog. Absence of normal cabin windows means that the crew could both be seated at the same level in a very slim fuselage completely covered in non-reflection radar-absorbent material.

Weapons

The first types of armament carried by helicopters were guns and bombs. From 1943 the Focke-Achgelis Fa 223 was tested with MG 15 machine guns and pairs of SC250 bombs of 551lb each. Indeed, many years were to elapse before other helicopters carried such a bombload. In the Korean War machines of the S-55 family carried tubes for launching unguided rockets, but it was not until the war in Algeria, ending in 1963, that helicopters were seriously used in large numbers as carriers of guns, rockets and bombs, and also the lately developed wire-guided missile with a hollow-charge warhead (not against armour but to kill people in rocky mountainous terrain).

Today, of course, a helicopter's weapons reflect its mission. Short of nuclear weapons and cruise missiles there are not many aerial weapons that are not carried by combat helicopters. Even the SAR (search and rescue) machine has a special sub-class known as "combat SAR", which is tasked with bringing back downed aircraft, special forces personnel or any other friendly people from enemy territory.

An increasing number of battlefield helicopters have sensors operating at laser (near-optical) wavelengths. The simplest such sensor is merely a receiver, able to detect and track a source of laser light of a compatible (similar) wavelength. Such a receiver can detect a target "illuminated" by a laser aimed by (for example) a friendly infantryman. The helicopter can then attack the target with a laser-homing missile, such as Hellfire. Alternatively, the helicopter can carry its own laser and do its own designation of targets. The obvious best solution, of course, is to try to use the same optical path for both optics and the laser, with a parallel IR channel, all incoming pictures being presented on a single big display. Typically, the display would show a radar and/or FLIR picture, perhaps both superimposed, while the laser would be used for precision ranging and missile guidance.

Several of the entries in this book mention NVGs (night-vision goggles). Such goggles look like miniature binoculars and are electro-optical devices which enormously intensify the stream of photons (light units) coming from the target at

Thus the CSAR machine has to be well protected with countermeasures and armour, and also to have firepower at the very least to "keep enemy heads down". Typically such firepower comprises pintle-mounted machine guns, or possibly guns of up to 20mm calibre or more fixed to fire ahead (or trainable through a limited arc). Back in the Vietnam War some early AH-1 Cobra gunships were fitted with chin turrets housing, as an alternative to a machine gun or 7.62mm Minigun, a 40mm grenade launcher. The most common grenade launcher was the Hughes/Ford Aeronutronic M129, part of the Emerson M28 turret, which could fire 40mm grenades at the rate of three hundred to four hundred per minute to a distance of 7,200ft (2,200m) with a very impressive degree of accuracy. Such projectiles were invariably highly effective, and it seems remarkable that they are seldom seen today.

Instead, chin turrets of modern helicopters invariably carry a gun only. Guns range in calibre from 5.56mm up to at least 30mm. Variations seem almost limitless. Many schemes have one or more guns fixed to fire ahead. The most powerful such installation is the twin-barrel GSh-30-2 fitted to the Mi-35P

and related Soviet attack transports. Dedicated anti-armour helicopters often have a powerful gun mounted in the chin position, often completely exposed, and aimed over a wide cone of fire by the CPG's control handgrips. In the AH-64A and Mi-28 the gun is of 30mm calibre. In the case of the Soviet helicopter the gun has a special higher rate of fire for use in the air-to-air role. In contrast, no gun is fitted to either the French or German anti-tank version of the Eurocopter Tiger, whereas the French HAP escort version does have a gun, a 30mm weapon which presumably could be aimed against air as well as ground targets. Even more curiously, Britain appears to have overlooked the need to develop guns for helicopters, with the result that we have to use whatever is available from France, Belgium or the USA. Britain has only one modern aircraft gun, the Aden 25, and in 1990 this was still not operational on its sole application, the RAF Harrier GR.5/7. On the other hand, one British company, Lucas Aerospace, has on its own initiative developed a versatile chin turret which originally mounted the long-lived (1916 design) Browning 0.5in (12.7mm) but now is available with several other types of gun.

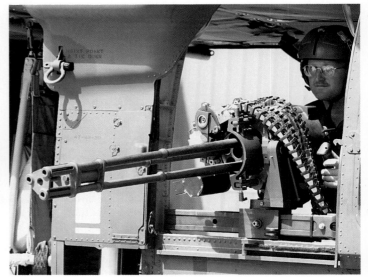

Above: Mounted in the main cabin to allow the maximum sweep of fire, this triple-barrel Gecal 50 12.7mm gun offers increased protection for its UH-60A Blackhawk platform. Linked or linkless feed ammunition can be used, and a rate of fire of 4,000 rpm is possible. A six-barrel model has exactly double the rate of fire of the model illustrated.

Left: Pivoted toward the camera, the AH-64A Apache's nose displays its triple cluster of sensors, namely the Pilot's Night Vision Sensor (PNVS) IR scanner (top); the night systems sensor scanner (middle left); and the Target Acquisition and Designation Sight (TADS) daylight scanner (middle right). The PNVS and TADS units are independently steerable.

Hellfire Cutaway

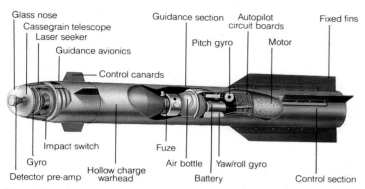

Labels: Glass nose, Cassegrain telescope, Laser seeker, Guidance avionics, Guidance section, Autopilot circuit boards, Fixed fins, Pitch gyro, Motor, Control canards, Impact switch, Fuze, Gyro, Air bottle, Yaw/roll gyro, Detector pre-amp, Hollow charge warhead, Battery, Control section

Above: Featuring a self-contained homing device, the Rockwell Hellfire *is the principle anti-tank missile carried by US Army AH-64As.*

Today hardly any helicopters carry bombs, so next to guns the longest-established weapons are rockets. The unguided but spin-stabilized rocket has been made by the million, with warheads designed to explode, penetrate armour, make smoke, burn with a brilliant light for illumination, burn with high IR output as a decoy or dispense millions of slivers of chaff. Most rockets have fins which unfold very quickly as soon as the rocket leaves the launch tube (a few are fired without tubes) to initiate and then sustain a rapid spin for stabilisation purposes. Other are spun by twisting the jet from the propulsion motor. Advantages are low cost and good "blanket" coverage, but accuracy of any individual rocket is rather poor. Important calibres include 37, 50, 57, 68, 70, 75, 80, 81, 100, 135 and 280mm.

Undoubtedly the primary weapon of the anti-armour helicopter is the guided missile, with a hollow-charge warhead capable (in theory) of piercing the heaviest tank armour. Sweden's BILL Missile has triggered a new generation of missiles deliberately designed not to hit the target but to fly just over the top, the warhead being so triggered that the hypervelocity jet punches down through the top of the hull or turret, which is much thinner than the frontal armour. In BILL's case the missile is automatically guided by signals sent along trailing wires from the launcher which continuously watches the position of a laser tracking signal transmitter in the missile, the computer processor always injecting a deliberate vertical offset to keep the missile 40in (1m) above the operator's line of sight.

Most other missiles are steered to hit the target squarely. Some of the latest missiles use electromagnetic radiation for precision guidance. For example the AT-6 "Spiral" carried by Soviet helicopters has a near-perfect form of unjammable radio guidance, while AGM-114 Hellfire, carried by the AH-64A Apache, homes automatically on targets designated (illuminated) by a compatible laser, such as that carried by the Apache. In contrast, the vast majority of anti-armour missiles currently deployed require that the human operator in the helicopter should see the target the whole time the missile is in flight — often a quarter of a minute or more — and steer the missile dead in line with the target throughout that time. As the pilot has to hold the helicopter as still as possible during this procedure it can be seen how lethal it is for the machine to have to expose itself to the enemy during each engagement.

Of course, in the ASW (anti-submarine warfare) role the principal weapons are the homing torpedo and the depth charge. A/S (anti-submarine) torpedoes are much smaller than those used against large surface ships, though their guidance has if anything to be even more sophisticated. Instead of merely running at a steady depth near the surface of the sea the A/S torpedo has to hit a target probably moving at high speed in three dimensions with agility rivalling that of a fighter aircraft. Some have electric propulsion, and others some form of high-energy chemical system driving propellers or a water jet. Most have passive or combined passive/active acoustic homing, steering always towards the noise from the target, while others are wire guided by signals sent from the sensor-equipped parent helicopter.

A typical air-launched depth charge is the British Mk 11. This, with tail fitted, has a length of 54.7in (1,390mm) and weighs 320lb (145kg), of which 176lb (80kg) is the HE warhead. The tail breaks off when the weapon hits the water to facilitate hydropneumatic arming, and subsequent detonation at the preset depth.

Several helicopters have also been equipped to sow mines, both at sea and, especially, over land. Sea mines are usually extremely large, so few helicopters can lay more than one, or two at most. In contrast, battlefield mines are much smaller and can be dispensed in large numbers. A typical installation is the Volcano system, designed for the UH-60A Black Hawk. It comprises four packages, two mounted on each side of the cabin, each package being able to fire 40 canisters, each in turn housing up to six of the Gator family of mines. The helicopter flies fast and low over the target area dispensing its 960 mines in such a way that they are randomly scattered over a wide area. Then the four empty racks are blown cleanly off the helicopter. Another minelaying system is the DAT from Tecnovar. A Lynx was used to demonstrate the DAT Model A dispenser, which can accommodate 64 magazines with a total of 1,536 anti-personnel mines, or 32 magazines housing a total of 128 anti-tank mines, or a mixture.

Sowing land minefields from the air would seem to be a major area of helicopter technology that has yet to be properly developed. The possibilities are obviously considerable, but proven systems are generally not yet available.

19

Aérospatiale SA 542 Gazelle

Though the first SA 340 prototype made its first flight as long ago as 7 April 1967, continual updating has kept it competitive, and it remains in limited production with well over 1,250 delivered. This total includes 294 made by Westland as part of the 1967 Anglo-French agreement, but not 220 built in Yugoslavia and 30 in Egypt.

Distinguished by its streamlined shape and shrouded multi-blade tail rotor (called a Fenestron), the Gazelle is a neat and quite agile machine with speed higher than most helicopters. In front, with a virtually perfect view, sits the pilot, who can have a second seat beside him. Behind can be a bench seat for three, which can be folded down to leave a flat floor for cargo. Virtually all Gazelles are equipped for flying at night or in bad weather, and many have the optional autopilot or dual flight controls, and the RAF and Royal Navy use Gazelles as helicopter pilot trainers. Many operators have the ambulance fit which adds two spineboards along the left side, for stretcher casualties, leaving room for an attendant on the right.

Origin: France.
Engine: One Turbomeca Astazou XIVM with max rating of 858shp.
Dimensions: Diameter of main rotor 34ft 6in (10.5m); length overall. (rotors turning) 39ft 3.3in (11.97m).
Weights: Empty (542L$_1$) 2,198lb (997kg); maximum loaded (542L$_1$) 4,409lb (2,000kg).
Performance: (542L$_1$, typical, max weight) maximum speed and maximum cruising speed 161mph (260km/h); hovering ceiling out of ground effect 7,775ft (2,370m); range at sea level 440 miles (710km).
Armament: Four (rarely six) HOT anti-tank missiles, or (Yugoslavia) four AT-3 Sagger anti-tank missiles and two SA-7 Grail air/air missiles; two 7.62mm machine guns or one 20mm GIAT M621 cannon firing ahead; provision for various rocket launchers including two launchers for thirty-six SNEB 68mm rockets or FZ 2.75in rockets; provision for GPMG or other gun mounted on pintle and fired from a side door.
History: First flight 7 April 1967, first delivery of 342M February 1980.

During the Falklands War many modifications, including the fitting of SNEB rocket launchers, were designed and cleared for service use by British Army Gazelles in a matter of three to five days, and Gazelles played a major role in the recovery of the islands, mainly in the liaison, front-line transport and casevac roles. Since then British Army Gazelle AH.1s have been fitted with the Ferranti AF 532 magnifying optical sight to fit them for scout duties, and the same sup-

plier's Aware-3 radar warning receivers are now added. Many other Gazelles around the world have similar stabilized optical sights and radar warning equipment. Some have the jetpipe upturned to reduce IR emission.

The latest versions are the SA 542L$_1$ and the 542M, the latter for the French Army ALAT. Recent customers, including the ALAT, have specified Decca Doppler navigation radar and the Crouzet Nadir self-contained navigation system, the SFIM PA85G autopilot and night-flying equipment. Egyptian Gazelles have the SFIM Osloh 1 laser designator for pointing out surface targets for ground artillery (or, in theory, for laser-homing missiles fired by any friendly platform). Current ALAT orders include 188 fitted with four HOT missiles and the APX M397 roof-mounted sight.*It should be noted that in 1990 Aérospatiale changed its numerical designations from the 300 series to the 500 series.

Left: The pilot of this Army Air Corps Gazelle AH.1 is looking into the eyepiece of the Ferranti AF 532 stabilized optical sight mounted on the roof. This sight has been designed so that a laser ranger, target market or missile guider could easily be added.

Below: though primarily designed for anti-armour operations, the ALAT (French Army Light Aviation Corps) SA 542Ms can also be armed for air-to-air operations. In this case, the usual armament of HOT anti-armour missiles has given way to a quartet of Matra Mistral infra-red homing AAMs, although as many as six could be carried.

Left: This Gazelle AH.1 has no missile sight, doppler or VHF, but is fitted with a GPMG on a pintle mount and two prominent ventral UHF communications antennae. The left door is shown removed.

Aérospatiale AS 532 Super Puma

Origin: France.
Engines: Two Turbomeca Makila IA1, each rated at 1,877shp.
Dimensions: Diameter of main rotor 51ft 2.2in (15.6m); (Mk II, 53ft 1.8in, 16.2m); length overall (rotors turning) 61ft 4.3in (18.7m).
Weights: (532B, M) empty 9,832lb (4,460kg); maximum 19,841lb (9,000kg), (with slung load) 20,615lb (9,350kg).
Performance: Maximum cruising speed 163mph (262km/h); hovering ceiling out of ground effect 5,415ft (1,650m); range at sea level (B) 384 miles (618km), (M) 523 miles (842km).
Armament: Naval 532F can carry one or two AM39 Exocet anti-ship missiles, or (ASW role) two light torpedoes plus ASW weapons; army B or M versions can carry various rocket launchers or guns, including two 7.62mm or one 20mm.
History: First flight (AS 332) 13 September 1978; (Mk II) 6 February 1987.

This versatile helicopter is an improved version of the SA 330 Puma, which first flew on 15 April 1965. A total of just over 700 Pumas has been built, including 11 assembled in Indonesia and (by early 1990) just over 150 in Romania, where small numbers are still being built.

The AS 532 Super Puma versions differ from their predecessor mainly in that the Turmo engines are replaced by the more powerful and more fuel-efficient Makila, new glassfibre rotor blades are fitted, together with a simpler retractable landing gear with single main wheels with greater energy absorption, a longer forward fuselage and nose, improved fin and tailplane profiles and increased fuel capacity. The Super was a success from the start, and by late 1989 the total ordered was nearing 350, though this includes civil versions. There is also a further improved Super Puma Mk II mentioned later.

The chief non-civil versions in use in 1990 are: the AS 532B$_1$, the standard military transport, carrying a crew of two and 21 troops or cargo; the 532F$_1$, naval version with deck-recovery system and folding tail rotor; and the 532M$_1$, similar to the B but with a cabin 30in (0.76m) longer to seat 25 troops, and with greater fuel capacity. Many Super Pumas have prominent Centrisep inlet filters which are essential for flight in sandy conditions. Another option is large boxes on the main landing gears and forward fuselage housing emergency rapid-inflating buoyancy bags.

The cockpit can be equipped for either one or two pilots, and in SAR (search and rescue) versions always has Bendix or RCA search radar mounted in the nose. In almost every Super Puma very comprehensive night and bad-weather navigation equipment is installed, and many customers have chosen the optional de-icing system, with engine inlet grills and electric heating mats along the leading edges of the main and tail rotor blades. Other customer options include a sling for external loads of up to 9,921lb (4,500kg), a fixed or retractable rescue hoist of 606lb (275kg) capacity, and interior furnishing for many missions including VIP, cargo, 21 to 25 troops or ambulance, the latter with six stretchers and 11 seated or nine stretchers and three seated.

The Super Puma Mk II has a new and enlarged main rotor with an improved hub and parabolic blade tips, a slightly longer rear fuselage, extra (optional) fuel tanks, a four-tube electronic flight instrument display and a digital autopilot. The new rotor enables gross weight to reach 20,945lb (9,500kg). The French Army expects to deploy 20 Mk IIs from 1995 as battlefield surveillance aircraft. Each will have the Orchidée radar, with a giant retractable rotating antenna under the rear fuselage. The antenna is nearly 17ft (5.2m) long, and when operating can present detailed pictures of vehicles and troops up to 62 miles (100km) behind a battlefront.

Below: The prototype Super Puma, with civil registration, first flew in September 1978. It can be seen that little damage would result from an emergency landing on the retracted landing gear. There is a bulged fairing (above the sponson) over the leg.

Right: Some customers have purchased examples of the AS 532F family, for naval use. This can carry up to two AM39 Exocet anti-ship missiles, as seen here. Most naval Super Pumas have Thomson-CSF Varan nose radar.

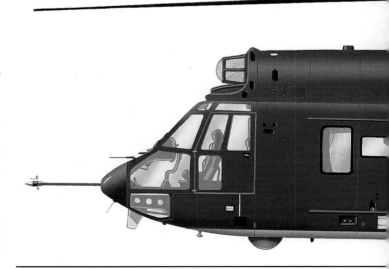

Above: Troops being landed by an AS 532B army version, with the short fuselage. This example has a simple anti-ice grille over each inlet, whereas the naval helicopter, left, has Centrisep sand/dust separators.

F-WZJA

Aérospatiale AS 555M₂ Ecureuil 2

Origin: France, licensed to Brazil.
Engines: (550) one 724shp Turbomeca Arriel 1D1 or 615shp Textron Lycoming LTS 101-600A-3; (555, most) two 420shp Allison 250-C20F, (555N) two 456shp Turbomeca TM 319.
Dimensions: Diameter of main rotor 35ft 0.8in (10.69m); length overall (rotors turning) 42ft 5.5in (12.94m).
Weights: (555M₂) Empty 3,020lb (1,370kg); max loaded 5,732lb (2,600kg).
Performance: Max cruising speed (550L₂) 151mph (243km/h), (555M₂) 137mph (221km/h); hovering ceiling out of ground effect (550L₂) 8,200ft (2,500m), (555M₂) 4,920ft (1,500m); range at sea level, no reserves (both similar) 430 miles (692km).
Armament: Very wide variety of fits including GIAT M621 20mm gun, FN twin 7.62mm gun pod, nine types of rocket launcher (UH-12 carries Avibras 7 × 70mm, or two homing torpedoes), or four HeliTOW missiles; 555N carries Mistral AAMs.
History: First flight (350) 27 June 1974, (355) 28 September 1979.

Aérospatiale developed the Ecureuil (squirrel) as a successor to the Alouette, which as a pioneer turbine helicopter sold in large numbers in 67 countries. The first version to fly was the AS 350, marketed in many versions with a single Turbomeca Arriel or Textron Lycoming LTS 101 engine, in each case of about 700shp. By 1990 more than 1,300 AS 350s had been delivered, including some equipped for anti-tank missile operations, search and rescue and other military tasks, a wide range of gun, rocket and missile armament being available.

More recently large-scale production has been undertaken of the twin-engined AS 555 family. Like the AS 350 this family has an advanced three-blade main rotor with a Starflex glassfibre hub incorporating a maintenance-free "ball-joint" of rubber and steel sandwich, eliminating all bearings. The tail rotor is not a Fenestron, though one has been tested on an Ecureuil. Typically the cabin contains two bucket seats at the front, with dual controls in pilot-training versions, and two two-seat benches behind. A large sliding door is fitted on each side and there are three baggage bays each with an external door. The landing gear is of the fixed skid type, customers having the option of emergency flotation gear.

The French Armée de l'Air is receiving 44 AS 555F₂ helicopters for surveillance of strategic bases, such as the ICBM silos on the Plateau d'Albion. Eight have the Allison engine and the remaining 36 the new TM 319 (see data). The

Below: The AS 550 has found favour with a number of armed services around the world, including those of six single-engined AS 550Bs currently in service with the Republic of Singapore Air Force. An armed variant of this model, known as AS 550L, is fitted with weapon "wings" and taller landing skids.

standard military model so far has been the AS 555M$_2$, with Allison engines. Optional equipment includes a 360° Bendix 1500 radar in the chin position, Crouzet Nadir Mk 10 navigation system, Crouzet Mk 3 MAD (anti-submarine anomaly detection) beneath the tailboom, SFIM autopilot, ESD doppler and auto-hold, radio altimeter, electric de-icing, rescue winch and provision for stretcher casualties. A major customer is Brazil which calls the helicopter by its Portuguese name, Esquilo. The Brazilian company Helibras has delivered considerably more than 200, many having Brazilian weapon fits. The chief versions for the Brazilian air force are designated CH-50 and TH-50 (armed and trainer single-engine) and CH-55 and VH-55 (armed and VIP twin-engine). The first 20 for the Brazilian navy have the designation UH-12, and have a weapon fit as described in the data.

Left: Easily distinguished by the double-engine configuration, the AS 555 represents a significant improvement in the Ecureuil's overall capabilities. Illustrated is an AS 555M$_2$, a variant which is equipped to carry a variety of missiles, rocket packs and guns, including the side-mounted GIAT M621 20mm lightweight, low recoil automatic gun, with a maximum rate of fire of 740 rounds per minute.

Below: Head-on aspect of an AS 555N armed with a brace of Matra Mistral air-to-air missiles and a side-mounted 20mm GIAT M 621 cannon. Under the new designations N will disappear, the only suffix letters being: A, armed; C, anti-tank; M, naval; S, armed naval (anti-ship or ASW); and U, utility. Other letters may, of course, be added in line with future military applications.

Agusta A 129 Mangusta

Origin: Italy.
Engines: Two Rolls-Royce RR1004, each rated at 881shp (1hr) or 1,035shp (20sec).
Dimensions: Diameter of main rotor 39ft 0.5in (11.9m); length overall (rotors turning) 46ft 10.5in (14.29m).
Weights: Empty (equipped) 5,575lb (2,529kg); max loaded 9,039lb (4,100kg).
Performance: Maximum speed (dash) 196mph (315km/h), (sustained) 161mph (259km/h); hovering ceiling out of ground effect 9,900ft (3,015m).
Armament: Four underwing attachments, each rated at 661lb (330kg); loads can include eight TOW 2 or HOT missiles, six Hellfire, various rocket launchers and gun pods (usually two 7.62, 12.7 or 20mm), and AIM-9L Sidewinder, Mistral, Javelin or Stinger AAMs.
History: First flight 15 September 1983; first delivery 1988.

Though it has some features in common with the widely used A 109 family of helicopters, the A 129 is slightly larger and much more powerful. It is a specialized anti-tank helicopter, the only one ever designed "from a clean sheet of paper" for this mission in Europe. The requirement of the Italian army for such a helicopter was issued in 1972, and the A 129 was approved in 1978. Following a prolonged development, manufacture of the first 15 production machines began in 1986, and in 1990 two squadrons, with 30 helicopters each, were being equipped, and a further 30 Mangustas were expected to be ordered to equip a third squadron.

As far as possible the Mangusta has the same mission capability as the AH-64A Apache, though it is smaller and very much less expensive. The entire aircraft has been designed to withstand strikes from projectiles of up to 12.7mm calibre, and the main rotor blades and numerous other parts have also shown "considerable tolerance" against hits from shells of 23mm calibre. The main rotor has elastomeric hub bearings, requiring no lubrication, and advanced carbon/Kevlar and Nomex honeycomb blades. Large areas of the

Left: Looking down on an A129 of the Italian army, This is the only anti-armour helicopter in production in Western Europe. A proposed multi-national upgraded version, the Tonal, has attracted little support.

airframe, including 45 per cent of the fuselage by weight, are made of composite materials, and access to equipment is made easy by removing large honeycomb panels.

The crew of two sit in tandem, the pilot being behind and much higher than the co-pilot/gunner. Each has an almost perfect view through a flat-plate bulletproof low-glint canopy. Hinged doors are on the right, blow-out side panels are provided for exit in emergency, and the fixed main gear and "crashworthy" seats absorb energy in seemingly unsurvivable impacts.

A particular feature of the A 129 is its exceedingly advanced avionics, all items being digital and linked to a MIL-STD-1553B bus, as is now specified for all future NATO aircraft. Navigation is assisted by a computer storing up to 100 waypoints, a pilot's night-vision system (helicopter IR night system), a forward-looking IR sensor mounted on a Ferranti stable platform in the nose, and and IHADSS (integrated helmet and display sighting system) for both crew. Italian army machines have the best suite of passive and active EW (electronic warfare) devices yet in service on any helicopter, including bus-linked radar and laser warning receivers, an IR sensor, radar and active IR jammers and a chaff/flare dispenser. The main rotor hub is equipped to mount an MMS

(mast-mounted sight), for IR/laser target acquisition, TOW tracking, laser ranging, laser designation for Hellfire and auto tracking of targets designated by co-operating lasers.

In 1988 one A 129 began flying with the LHX engine, the LHTEC T800. This could power an advanced multinational version called the Tonal.

Above: Prototype of the A129, first flown in 1983. Development has proved successful throughout.

Below: Side elevation of a production Mangusta of the Italian army. The name means Mongoose.

Agusta-Bell AB 212ASW

Costruzione Aeronautiche Giovanni Agusta obtained its first licence to make Bell helicopters in 1952. Since then many hundreds have been delivered in many versions, including large numbers of Italian-built variants of the familiar Bell ''Huey''. Current production is centred on the 212ASW and also on the 412SP and Griffon. The 412 and Griffon have a new four-blade rotor and many other changes, the new rotor allowing the cruising speed (rather slow in other models) to be increased to 144mph (232km/h). Griffons are in production for almost every conceivable military or naval purpose, though most are assigned to liaison, scouting, battlefield support, casevac or electronic-warfare missions.

The 212 has been in production much longer. All differ from earlier Huey models in having the 1,875hp PT6T engine, which has two power sections, giving what amounts to twin-engine safety. Agusta has delivered AB 212 helicopters to a very large number of countries, even the specialized 212ASW having sold to the tune of some 130 examples. Of course the 212ASW is wholly marinized for operation in a salt-water

Origin: Italy.
Engines: One 1,875shp Pratt & Whitney Canada PT6T-6 Turbo TwinPac (single-engine rating, 970shp for 30min).
Dimensions: Diameter of main rotor 48ft 0in (14.63m); length overall (rotors turning) 57ft 1in (17.4m).
Weights: Empty 5,800lb (2,630kg), empty with mission equipment (typical) 7,540lb (3,420kg); max loaded 11,176lb (5,070kg).
Performance: Maximum cruising speed 115mph (185km/h); hovering ceiling out of ground effect (at 10,500lb) 1,300ft (396m); range (typical) 382 miles (615km).
Armament: ASV mission, typical two Sea Skua, Marte Mk 2 or AS.12 missiles; ASW mission, two Motofides 244AS or Mk 44/46 torpedoes or any of several ASV missiles.
History: First flight (212) April 1969, (412) August 1979.

environment, and, though de-icing is not normally fitted, night and bad-weather flight is possible. The cockpit can have single or dual controls, with a hydraulically powered automatic flight control system which provides for automatic approach to a low-level hover irrespective of wind. Equipment can be provided for up to seven passengers, or cargo or, with a 600lb (272kg) rescue hoist, four stretcher patients. Slung loads can be carried up to 5,000lb (2,722kg). With ASW or ASV equipment the cabin room and payload are limited.

Two chief missions are ASV (anti-surface vessel) or ASW

(anti-submarine warfare). In the ASV role a Ferranti Seaspray radar is carried above the fuselage, together with automatically linked navigation aids and particularly comprehensive Selenia or Elettronica ECM (electronic countermeasures) systems. Ship attack is normally performed with the Sea Skua or Marte Mk 2 missile. The 212 ASW can also be equipped with different radar and real-time target data transmission for the passive midcourse guidance of Otomat 2 cruise missiles launched by friendly ships.

In the ASW role equipment the Bendix ASQ-13B/F variable-depth sonar is used in conjunction with a comprehensive navigation system which allows the sensor to be dipped at any desired point in a complex pattern. Tacan, UHF direction finding, a radar transponder and radar altimeter are also essential. Other equipment includes rapid-inflating emergency pontoons and external auxiliary fuel tanks. ASW weapons are listed in the data box.

Below: Side elevation of an AB 212ASW of the Italian Aviazione per la Marina (navy). Not surprisingly this was the largest customer, with sixty-six equipping units aboard frigates, destroyers and the Vittorio Veneto ASW carrier. Note the large housing for the radar.

Right: Unlike many ASW helicopters, the AB 212ASW normally uses a dipping (dunking) sonar. The Bendix equipment used has a maximum operating depth of 450ft (137m). This helicopter has a different search radar from the one shown below.

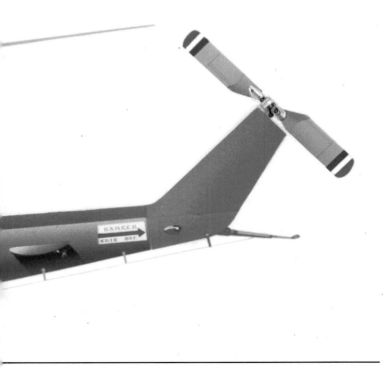

Bell UH-1H Iroquois ('Huey")

Origin: USA.
Engine: One Textron Lycoming T53-L-13 rated at 1,400shp.
Dimensions: Diameter of main rotor 48ft 0in (14.63m); length overall (rotors turning) 57ft 9.7in (17.62m).
Weights: Empty 5,210lb (2,363kg); max loaded 9,500lb (4,309kg).
Performance: Maximum and cruising speed (same) 127mph (204km/h); hovering ceiling out of ground effect 4,000ft (1,220m); range (typical, no reserves) 245 miles (394km).
Armament: Large numbers of US Army UH-1 helicopters operated with either fixed or pintle-mounted M60 (7.62mm) machine guns, and various rocket pods, notably including the 19-tube 2.75in launcher.
History:
First flight (Model 205) 16 August 1961; first delivery (UH-1H) September 1967.

The Korean War of 1950-53 identified a need for a specially designed utility helicopter to fly front-line supply missions, casevac and similar duties. The result was the Bell XH-40 of 1956, a simple machine with an engine of just under 700hp and six seats. Today, more than 15,000 sales later, the XH-40 has been developed into twin-engined Model 214s of 3,300hp seating 20, Cobra armed helicopters which behave like fighters and, most numerous of all, the UH-1H and many close relatives, which are the XH-40's direct descendants.

The Model 212 has already been described under licensee Agusta. In contrast the Model 205, of which the UH-1H is the most numerous member, still retains the same T53 engine as fitted to the XH-40, though today it is more powerful. The main rotor is still a two-blade semi-rigid "teetering" pattern, much as it was 35 years ago, though the blades are larger and made of new composite materials. A small pivoted tailplane is linked to the pilot's cyclic control to increase the permissible centre of gravity range. Nearly all "Hueys" (the name stems from the original 1962 designation of HU-1) have a simple landing gear comprising fixed tubular skids, though inflatable nylon bags can be added.

Over the years both the payload and the cabin volume of the Huey have increased. The UH-1H, no fewer than 4,945 of which were produced by Bell (including 3,573 for the US Army) and more than 1,000 by licensees, was the final production version of the Model 205 family. It has seats for a pilot and 11 to 14 troops, or up to 3,880lb (1,759kg) of cargo or six stretcher casualties and an attendant. Fuji of Japan has developed various features incorporated in the Advanced 205A-1, among them an uprated transmission, more powerful T53 engine and, significantly, a link called LIVE (liquid

inertial vibration eliminator). This is inserted between the transmission and fuselage to cut vibration by 80 per cent and increase cruising speed to 150mph (241km/h). The US Army may be among customers who could convert their existing machines to 205A-1 standard, although it is by no means certain that this option will be acted upon.

Though most military UH-1H and related helicopters are unarmed, various weapon fits were commonly used in Vietnam, and some operators still have armament installed. About 220 US Army machines have been converted to UH-1V medevac standard, with hoist, glideslope and radar altimeter, while an enormous upgrade programme is planned to enable at least 2,700 improved UH-1H helicopters to remain in front-line US Army service beyond year 2000.

Below: Final production version of the "Huey" family, the Bell UH-1H has been adopted by a large number of foreign customers, in addition to forming a large part of the US Army's helicopter transport force. This example is one of a large number manufactured in Nationalist China (Taiwan).

Right: Over 200 US Army UH-1Hs have been converted to undertake medevac tasks. Known as UH-1Vs, they can carry up to six litters and a medical attendant in the main cabin, with easy access via the large, aft-sliding door. The large Red Cross symbol clearly identifies the UH-1V's role.

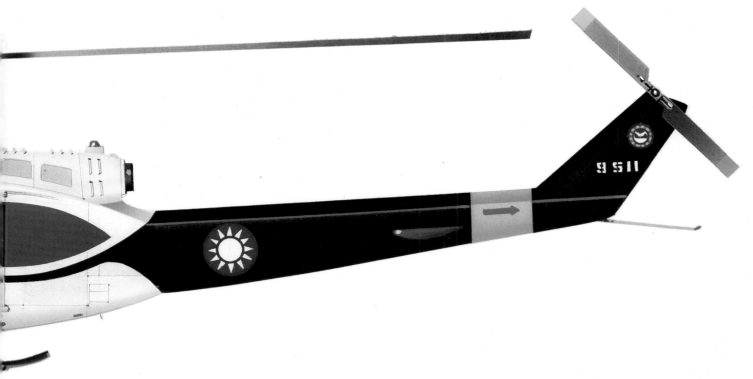

Bell OH-58D

Origin: USA.
Engine: One 650shp Allison 250-C30R.
Dimensions: Diameter of main rotor 35ft 0in (10.67m); length overall (rotors turning) 42ft 2in (12.85m).
Weights: Empty 2,825lb (1,281kg); max loaded 4,500lb (2,041kg).
Performance: Maximum speed 147mph (237km/h); hovering ceiling out of ground effect 11,200ft (3,415m); range (no reserve) 345 miles (556km).
Armament: (AH-58D) four Hellfire anti-tank missiles or two 0.5in (12.7mm) gun pods and two 7 × 2.75in rocket launchers, in each case with up to four Stinger air-to-air missiles.
History: First flight (OH-4A) 8 December 1962, (OH-58D) 6 October 1983.

The background to this helicopter is rather involved. It began as the Bell OH-4A for the US Army LOH (light observation helicopter) competition of 1961. This lost to the Hughes OH-6 (predecessor of the McDonnell Douglas Defender). Bell redesigned the OH-4 as the civil JetRanger, and in 1968 the US Army had second thoughts and ordered an immediate 2,200 JetRangers as the OH-58A Kiowa. Since then the availability of more powerful Allison engines and other factors have led to upgraded versions, such as 585 converted to OH-58C configuration with a 420hp engine, flat-plate nonglint canopy, IR protection, new night vision devices and improved instruments and avionics. In 1981 Bell's Model 406 was announced winner of the AHIP (Army helicopter improvement programme), resulting in today's OH-58D. The name Kiowa is no longer used, and in fact the Armed OH-58D version is unofficially the AH-58D Warrior.

So far all OH-58Ds are rebuilds of early OH-58A helicopters. The D version is such a big advance that it can be regarded as totally new. The engine is the C30R version, with a centrifugal compressor, giving greatly enhanced power and economy and requiring a new transmission uprated to 609shp. The rotor is a new ''soft in plane'' type with not two but four blades, of composite construction. The most prominent change is the addition of an MMS (mast-mounted sight) with a large ball housing a × 12 magnification TV camera, auto-focusing imaging IR sensor for night use and a laser rangefinder and target designator, the whole ball having automatic inflight boresighting and target tracking. Avionics are also completely new, including not only the new sensor displays but colour multifunction displays for horizontal and vertical situation, all these and the communications controls being on ''hands-on'' stick switches. Navigation aids include inertial and doppler systems, and crew equipment includes NVGs (night vision goggles).

The AH-58D is being delivered to SOF (Special Operations Forces) units. Among upgrades are the weapons listed in the specification, uprated engine for higher continuous power and an active IR jammer. Further improvements planned for all D models include both radar and laser warning, chaff/flare dispensers, IR jammer, optical enhancements, a GPS (global positioning system) receiver, digital data loader and chemical/biological masks for the crew.

Left: An OH-58D with MMS and full armament, the latter in this case comprising a rocket launcher and 7.62mm gun pod with large magazine.

Right: One of the oldest Kiowas — the sixth production OH-58A. With its serial number prefixed by an O, this helicopter is shown to be over ten years old.

Below: An AHIP OH-58D. Of course, the large MMS ball does not rotate, except in order to be aimed towards different battlefield targets.

Bell AH-1 Cobra Family

Origin: USA.
Engine(s): (AH-1E/F/P/S) one 1,800shp Textron Lycoming T53-703, (T) 1,970shp Pratt & Whitney Canada T400-402 twin unit, (W) two 1,723shp General Electric T700-401.
Dimensions: Diameter of main rotor (most) 48ft 0in (14.63m), (latest P) 44ft 0in (13.41m); length overall (rotors turning) (P) 53ft 1in (16.18m), (W) 58ft 0in (17.68m).
Weights: Empty (P) 6,598lb (2,993kg), (W) 10,200lb (4,627kg); max loaded (P) 10,000lb (4,536kg), (W) 14,750lb (6,690kg).
Performance: Maximum speed (P) 141mph (227km/h), (W, also cruising speed) 175mph (282km/h); hovering ceiling out of ground effect (P) not published, (W) 3,000ft (914m); range at sea level (P, 8% reserve) 315 miles (507km), (W, no reserve) 395 miles (635km).
Armament: (P) eight TOW missiles, and universal turret with 20mm or 30mm gun, (W) eight Hellfire or TOW missiles, turret with M197 20mm gun and very side range of other stores including two AIM-9L Sidewinder air/air missiles.
History: First flight (prototype) 7 September 1965, (W) 16 November 1983.

In the mid-1950s the US Army was urgently trying to assist Lockheed develop the AH-56A Cheyenne, an armed helicopter of awesome complexity. Meanwhile, Bell spent its own money developing a simpler armed helicopter based on the dynamic parts (engine, transmission and rotors) of the familiar UH-1. The US Army cancelled the Cheyenne and bought hundreds of AH-1 HueyCobras for use in Vietnam. Today the total number built is nearing 2,000, in a bewildering number of versions.

All variants have essentially the same narrow but deep fuselage, with tandem seating for the CPG (co-pilot/gunner) in the nose and the pilot above and to the rear. All have a two-blade rotor, though the blades differ greatly between versions. Early types have metal blades of 21in chord, the latest AH-1Ps (from No 67) have composite blades of 30in chord and the far more powerful AH-1W has rectangular blades of 33in chord. In 1989 flight testing began of the AH-1BW with the completely new four-blade bearingless research rotor.

The original mass-produced model was the AH-1G for the US Army, with the 1,100hp T53-11 engine, four weapon stations under the mid-mounted stub wings, and various chin turrets mounting such weapons as the 7.62mm Minigun or 40mm grenade launcher. All have been modified, initially into various forms of AH-1Q with TOW missiles, then into various forms of AH-1S with the 1,800hp Dash-703 engine, night equipment, IR suppressed jetpipe, IR jammer, three-barrel M197 cannon, radar warning receiver, laser ranger and tracker and IR-based sighting and helmet display systems. The AH-1P are newly built, with non-glint flat-plate canopies

(which give more pilot headroom), new cockpit and improved communications. The AH-1E came next, basically a P with more electric power and enhanced armament including a universal 20/30mm turret. Then came the AH-1F, with 32 new or improved avionics items, as well as the new rotor blades and better protection against gunfire.

Losses in Vietnam prompted the Marines to fit the T400 Twin Pac, giving twin-engine safety. The result was the AH-1J SeaCobra, which was developed into the AH-1T with TOW missiles and a ventral fin, and this in turn led to the AH-1W SuperCobra, with tremendous increase in power and capability (see specification). The Marines have 44 of a planned force of 78, and also intend to convert their 39 AH-1Ts to "Super" standard.

Though by far the largest user of the AH-1 is the US Army, followed by the Marine Corps, several other countries are important customers. The first and largest foreign buyer was Israel. Other important sales have been made to Iran (it ordered 202 in pre-revolutionary days of the Shah), Spain, Pakistan, Jordan, South Korea, Thailand and (locally assembled) Japan.

Below: Latest members of the US Army Cobra family, the AH-1E and -1F are outwardly almost identical. Points to note include the M197 gun, flat-plate canopy and infra-red active jammer.

Right: Identifiable by its two large engines, the Marines' AH-1W keeps the original type of rounded cockpit canopy. At present, the only version of the HueyCobra armed with the AGM-114 Hellfire missile.

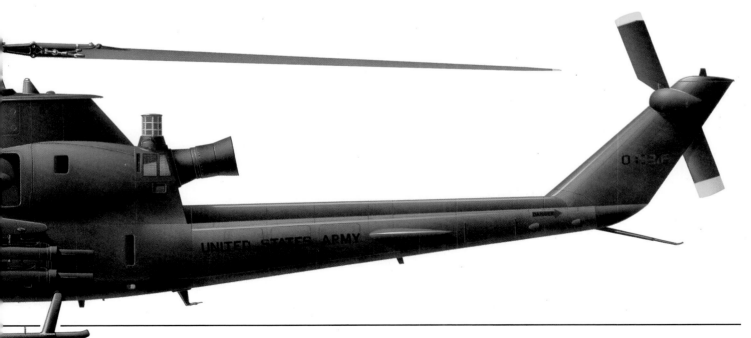

Boeing Helicopters CH-46E Sea Knight

Origin: USA.
Engines: Two 1,870shp General Electric T58-16.
Dimensions: Diameter of main rotors 50ft 0in (15.24m); length overall (rotors turning) 84ft 4in (25.70m).
Weights: Empty 13,342lb (6,051kg); max loaded 23,300lb (10,569kg).
Performance: Max speed 168mph (270km/h); hovering ceiling out of ground effect 5,100ft (1,554m); range with full load 230 miles (370km).
Armament: Usually none.
History: First flight (Model 107) April 1958, (CH-46A prototype) 27 August 1959.

The development of gas-turbine engines revolutionised the helicopter. In the mid-1950s two American engines in the 1,000hp class, the T53 and T58, enabled two very important twin-engined helicopters to be designed, the Sikorsky S-61 Sea King and the Vertol Model 107 Sea Knight. The Model 107 was noteworthy in that it had a long unobstructed cabin running almost the whole length. Right at the back were the two engines, and these drove a transmission connected to tandem three-blade rotors, one at each end of the helicopter. The landing gear, of the fixed tricycle type, mounted the twin-wheel main gears on sponsons, deep stub wings which not only house fuel but also provide stability should the

helicopter alight on water (though it was not specifically designed to be amphibious). One factor making sustained water operations difficult was that the whole rear end of the fuselage was made in the form of a powered ramp door, which allows bulky cargo and even light vehicles to go straight into the hold. There is another door at the front on the right side, with integral steps. Pilot and co-pilot sit side-by-side in the

Below: A CH-46E of the US Marine Corps, by far the most important user of this tandem-rotor transport. Despite major update and rebuild programmes the external appearance has hardly altered over the years. Apart from paint schemes the main change has been the addition of flotation bags (not fitted to this example).

extreme nose. The relatively capacious main cabin can accommodate up to 26 troops and their equipment, or it can house a payload of up to 10,000lb (4,536kg).

Large numbers of Type 107 helicopters were sold, including Canadian CH-113 Labrador and CH-113A Voyageur machines, today used in upgraded forms primarily for the SAR (search and rescue) role, Swedish HKP-4s powered by Rolls-Royce Gnome engines used mainly in the ASW and minesweeping roles, and many kinds of KV-107 and 107II helicopters made under licence by Kawasaki in Japan. By far the biggest customer was the US Marine Corps which, with the Navy, purchased 624 of various versions between 1964 and 1971. Between 1977 and 1986 Boeing Helicopters upgraded 273 Sea Knights to today's standard CH-46E configuration, with Dash-16 engines, a crash-resistant fuel system, impact-attenuating seats and many other changes. More recently Boeing has been putting the same helicopters, and some earlier models, through a safety, reliability and maintainability pro-

gramme to fit them for service beyond year 2000. A major change is to fit glassfibre blades, but there are many other changes to the avionics, flight controls, electrics, landing gear, rotor drive and airframe. From 1990 a further upgrade will be to add rapid-inflation emergency flotation bags, and 169 CH-46Es may also be given enhanced fuel capacity.

Right: Assault troops can be inserted by abseiling, either as shown in the photograph or from the side door.

Right: US Marines race into action after being air landed from a Sea Knight during a "hot" landing. Up to 26 fully-equipped troops can be carried, in the main cabin.

Boeing Helicopters CH-47 Chinook

When the US Army evaluated the original Vertol Model 107 it recognised the advantages of the tandem-rotor layout, with a completely unobstructed full-length cabin able to accept bulky cargo or even vehicles driven in at the rear. Obviously, provided an engine was available, the same idea could be scaled up to provide a cargo helicopter of far greater capability. Vertol, now called Boeing Helicopters, proposed this in the Model 114 of March 1959. This was quickly accepted, and the first production 114 was handed over to the Army in August 1962, with the designation CH-47A Chinook. Like all subsequent Chinooks, it was powered by two Textron Lycoming T55 engines mounted in pods outside the airframe on each side of the large fin-like pylon carrying the rear three-blade rotor. Fuel, in the latest versions 858gal (3,899litres),

Origin: USA (also made in Italy and Japan).
Engines: Two Textron Lycoming T55-712, rated at 3,750shp and with 4,500shp available in emergency.
Dimensions: Diameter of main rotors 60ft 0in (18.29m); length overall (rotors turning) 99ft 0in (30.18m).
Weights: Empty 22,784lb (10,335kg); max loaded 54,000lb (24,494kg).
Performance: Max speed at sea level (50,000lb, 22,680kg) 171mph (276km/h); hovering ceiling out of ground effect (50,000lb, 22,680kg) 6,100ft (1,860m); combat radius (not range) for external payload of 22,173lb (10,057kg) with 20min reserves, 115 miles (185km).
Armament: Usually none.
History: First flight (prototype) 21 September 1961, (CH-47C) 14 October 1967, (CH-47D) 11 May 1979.

is carried in large fairings along the lower sides of the fuselage which also carry the two front and two rear units of the landing gear. At the front is the side-by-side cockpit, with a jump seat for a combat commander or crew chief. The main cabin measures 99in wide at the floor and 78in high, and can be

Left: The latest Chinooks have three external payload hooks. A single load, such as this M198-towed 155mm howitzer, has to be slung from the centre hook so as to maintain the centre of gravity.

Below: Among the export customers for the Chinook is the Royal Moroccan Air Force. Eight of these helicopters were supplied, all having been built under licence in Italy by Elicotteri Meridionali.

equipped for up to 55 troops with equipment, or 24 stretcher casualties plus two attendants, or vehicles or cargo, the latter being allowed to project out through the open rear ramp door (provided centre of gravity is not beyond the aft limit).

The US Army received 732 Chinooks of CH-47A, B and C models, each with progressively better performance and flight characteristics. Many were lost in South-East Asia, but since 1982 Boeing has remanufactured 472 Chinooks to the current CH-47D standard. The process involves stripping machines down to the bare airframe and rebuilding with Dash-712 engines, new-profile blades of glassfibre, an uprated transmission, a new cockpit, advanced flight controls and hydraulics, totally upgraded avionics, adding a Solar gas-turbine APU (auxiliary power unit) to operate systems on the ground, fitting various survivability and defensive systems, a pressure fuelling socket and triple hooks for heavy external loads. The RAF, which are among many customers having their Chinooks upgraded, can hang 28,000lb (12,700kg) on the centre hook and 20,000lb (9,072kg) on the front and rear (but of course not all three together). Whereas the CH-47A

had a maximum payload of 11,000lb (4,990kg), today's CH-47D flies faster and has over twice the payload.

The latest version is the MH-47E for US Special Operations Forces. These have 4,110shp T55 engines and comprehensive equipment for "penetration" missions.

Right: A Boeing Helicopters CH-47C, a variant now being upgraded for the US Army as the CH-47D.

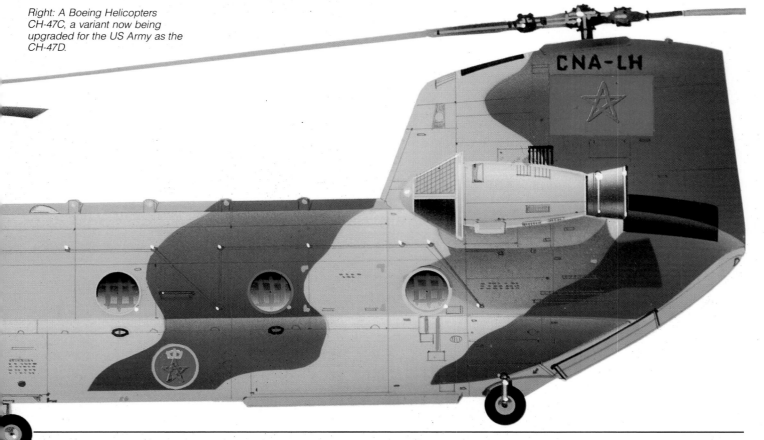

EH Industries EH101

Origin: Jointly UK/Italy.
Engines: Three General Electric T700: (naval) 1,714shp T700-401A, (military) 1,920shp CT7-6A.
Dimensions: Diameter of main rotor 61ft 0in (18.59m); length overall (rotors turning) 74ft 10in (22.81m).
Weights: Empty (naval) 15,700lb (7,121kg); equipped weight (naval) 20,500lb (9,298kg); max loaded (naval) 29,830lb (13,530kg).
Performance: Average cruising speed 184mph (296km/h); ferry range (military transport, with extra internal fuel) 1,301 miles (2,094km).
Armament: (naval) four homing torpedoes (Marconi Sting Ray for UK, Motofides 244AS for Italy), or six/eight Sea Skua or Marte Mk 2 anti-ship missiles in ASV role; (military) normally none.
History: First flight (first of nine pre-production aircraft) 9 October 1987.

This programme began in early 1977 when the British MoD (Navy) completed prolonged studies for an SKR (Sea King replacement) helicopter, with particular emphasis on the ASW mission. In 1978 the Westland WG.34 was selected for this task, but the Italian naval aviation had a similar need and in 1980 Westland decided to collaborate with Agusta, forming EHI, which stands for Elicotteri Helicopter Industries, giving the name of the product in both languages. Since then the EH101 has been defined in complete detail in several forms, and a manufacturing programme has been established for production for the Royal Navy, Italian Marina and Canadian Navy, and for planned transport versions for the RAF (on behalf of the British Army) and for civilian customers.

Though the EH101 is in most respects slightly smaller than the Sea King, which makes it easier to operate from cramped ship decks, it has about 50 per cent more power (having three engines instead of two, incidentally with much better fuel economy), and a European consortium is trying to displace the original US engine with a later design offering much greater power and even better fuel economy. This engine, the Rolls-Royce Turbomeca RTM 322, is rated at 2,312shp and has several technical advantages, but in early 1990 it had not been ordered to power the EH101.

Right: This side profile shows the appearance of an EH101 of the Italian navy, operating in the ASW role. From this side two of the three jetpipes can be seen, but these may later be suppressed to reduce the IR signature.

As the most urgently needed version the ASW/naval variant is designed to operate from 3,500-ton frigates in gale force winds and severe sea states, yet to carry out demanding search/attack missions far from its parent vessel on missions lasting 5 hours in the target area. Of course, all avionics are digital, linked to a 1553B bus, including (in the Royal Navy version, named Merlin) Ferranti Blue Kestrel radar, as well as sonobuoys, dipping sonar and exceptionally capable processing systems. Another mission will be OTH (over the horizon) surveillance, target tracking and midcourse guidance of missiles fired by friendly warships. The Royal Navy require 50 Merlins (though in early 1990 said it might cut its buy to only 25), while the Italian Navy requires 42 and the Canadian Navy between 30 and 50, in each case with different role equipment.

The utility version has a capacious hold for 30 equipped troops, or 16 stretchers and a medical team or cargo loads up to 15,000lb (6,804kg). Vehicles can be driven in through the rear ramp door, 6ft (1.83m) high and 98in (2.49m) wide. All versions have retractable tricycle landing gear, comprehensive electronic-warfare systems and full de-icing, while naval variants have automatic power folding of the five-blade main rotor and of the tail.

Above: The second prototype of the EH101 was assembled in Italy. In early 1990 the first utility transport version with a rear ramp door (the seventh prototype) began flight testing.

Eurocopter Tiger/Tigre

Origin: Joint project by France and West Germany.
Engines: Two 1,285shp MTU/Turbomeca/Rolls-Royce MTR 390.
Dimensions: Diameter of main rotor 42ft 7.8in (13.0m); length overall (rotors turning) about 51ft 8in (15.75m).
Weights: (Model not stated) basic empty 7,275lb (3,330kg); max loaded 11,685-12,346lb (5,300-5,600kg).
Performance: (Estimated at 11,905lb/5,400kg) max cruising speed 155-174mph (250-280km/h); hovering ceiling out of ground effect, over 6,561ft (2,000m); endurance 2hr 50min.
Armament: HAP, chin turret with GIAT 30781 30mm gun, four Mistral AAMs and two SNEB 22 × 68mm rocket launchers; PAH-2, eight HOT 2 and four Stinger 2 AAMs (later planned to replace HOT by eight Euromissile DG Trigat 'fire and forget' IR homing missiles); HAC, eight HOT 2 and four Mistral AAMs (with the possibility of later replacing HOT by Trigat).
History: First flight scheduled for spring 1991 and the second prototype some time in 1992.

Few aircraft in history have taken so long to emerge as this family of three basically similar helicopters to be developed by France and West Germany. Exactly 20 years will have elapsed between the first joint design by Aérospatiale and MBB and the first delivery to a customer in 1997 (provided that there are no more delays).

Originally Aérospatiale was collaborating with Westland on a "gunship" Lynx, and MBB with Agusta. In 1978 the Franco-German alliance was established, together with three versions of the helicopter today known as the Tiger. The HAP (Hélicoptère d'Appui Protection) is an escort and fire-support version for the French army, to be delivered from 1997. The PAH-2 (Panzerabwehr-Hubschrauber 2nd generation) is an anti-armour version for the West German army. The HAC (Hélicoptère Anti-Char) is the corresponding French model, which like PAH-2 is scheduled to begin deliveries from 1998.

General layout is similar to that of the Apache or Mangusta, though, amazingly, the pilot is seated in the nose and the co-pilot/gunner above and to the rear. Indeed until recently the German anti-tank version even had all its sensors mounted in the nose, forcing the pilot to expose the whole helicopter to the enemy! Even today the pilot's FLIR (forward-looking IR) night viewing system is in the nose. In the HAP the sensors — which are broadly similar to other versions in comprising an FLIR, TV, direct magnifying optics and laser ranger — are on the cockpit roof, just in front of the rotor.

Features include a relatively small main rotor with four composite blades, a fuselage and stub wings mainly of carbon fibre, with fairings of glassfibre or Kevlar, a complex tail with a swept fin, underfin, tailplane and two auxiliary fins, and fixed tailwheel landing gear (designed to withstand a vertical rate of descent up to 20ft/6m per second, compared with 33ft/10m per second for the rival A129). The rotors and transmission are to be designed to withstand 12.7mm hits, and parts of the fuselage are to be survivable against 23mm strikes.

Leadership in the project is shared. Eurocopter GmbH, which manages the project in Munich, is a wholly owned subsidiary of Eurocopter GIE in Paris, and the executive authority is the German Federal defence procurement agency. The supposed requirements, which have not changed much since 1977, are for 75 HAPs, 212 PAH-2s and 140 HACs. In 1990 Westland of the UK signed an agreement to participate in the event of some version of the Tiger being selected for the UK (but Westland has similar agreements on the Tonal based on the A129 and also on the Apache).

Below: During the Tiger's long development, its appearance has changed considerably. This profile shows what the anti-tank HAC/PAH-2 looked like from 1981 to 1983. By 1984 the backseat co-pilot/gunner (weapons system operator) had had a windscreen inserted ahead of his console.

Right: At each development stage, this full-scale mock-up (of the German PAH-2) has been modified to portray the latest configuration. The mast-mounted sight was agreed in 1987. The jetpipes are infra-red-suppressed, using ram air to provide cooling and thus lower the engine's heat signature.

Kaman SH-2G Super Seasprite

Designed in the 1950s, the SH-2 Seasprite has had a remarkably long active career. Today new examples are being manufactured and tired used specimens being refurbished and updated, and examples will certainly be in service in year 2000. Not least of the remarkable features is that the SH-2 began life with a single T58 engine of 1,000shp, was re-engined with two T58s of 1,250shp each and is now being built with two T700 engines of 1,723shp each, giving almost three and a half times the original installed power!

The original US Navy requirement of 1956 called for a high-speed utility helicopter able to operate from small ship decks carrying cargo, personnel and on rescue missions. Kaman's answer was a helicopter of notably neat and streamlined appearance, with a finely profiled fuselage and a tailwheel landing gear with fully retractable main units, each with twin wheels. Of course, because of its age, the SH-2 has a traditional riveted light-alloy airframe, but the main rotor in the

Origin: USA.
Engines: (F) Two 1,350shp General Electric T58-8, (G) two 1,723shp General Electric T700-401.
Dimensions: Diameter of main rotor (G) 44ft 4in (13.51m); length overall (rotors turning) 52ft 9in (16.08m).
Weights: Empty (F) 7,055lb (3,200kg), (G) 7,680lb (3,483kg); max loaded (F) 12,808lb (5,810kg), (G) 13,900lb (6,305kg).
Performance: Max speed (both) 165mph (265km/h); cruising speed 138mph (222km/h); hovering ceiling out of ground effect (G) 15,600ft (4,755m); max range (G) 645 miles (1,038km).
Armament: (ASW mission) one or two Mk 46 or Mk 50 torpedoes, eight Mk 25 smoke markers.
History: First flight (HU2K-1) 2 July 1959, (YSH-2G) late 1984.

latest version, the SH-2G, has four blades which, together with their unusual trailing-edge servo flap controls, are of composite construction. These give improved performance, as well as a service life of 10,000 hours.

It was in 1967 that Seasprites were retrofitted with twin engines, and they later underwent further modification to fit them for the LAMPS (light airborne multi-purpose system) mission. This added to the basic utility/SAR mission ASW (anti-submarine warfare) and ASST (anti-ship surveillance

Right: Though this SH-2F differs in many respects from latest G model, only obvious change is in size of engines. By 1990, several foreign customers for the Seasprite were appearing, Portugal among them.

and targeting). The result was an exceptionally versatile machine, with a cabin able to carry cargo, an external sling for a load of 4,000lb (1,814kg), seats for four passengers or two stretcher patients or, in the ASW role, for one passenger or stretcher casualty together with a side launcher for 15 sonobuoys, plus surveillance radar and a towed MAD (magnetic-anomaly detector). In any role comprehensive night and all-weather avionics are carried, together with an ESM (electronic surveillance measures) and a radar warning system, a chaff dispenser and a 600lb (272kg) rescue hoist.

Apart from the new main-rotor blades the SH-2G introduces the T700 engine. This enhances performance, and in particular extends the range (partly by better fuel economy and partly by enabling three tanks to be carried). The G model introduces digital avionics, all tied to a 1553B bus, items including a new acoustic processor and multifunction display for the tactical co-ordinator and sensor operator.

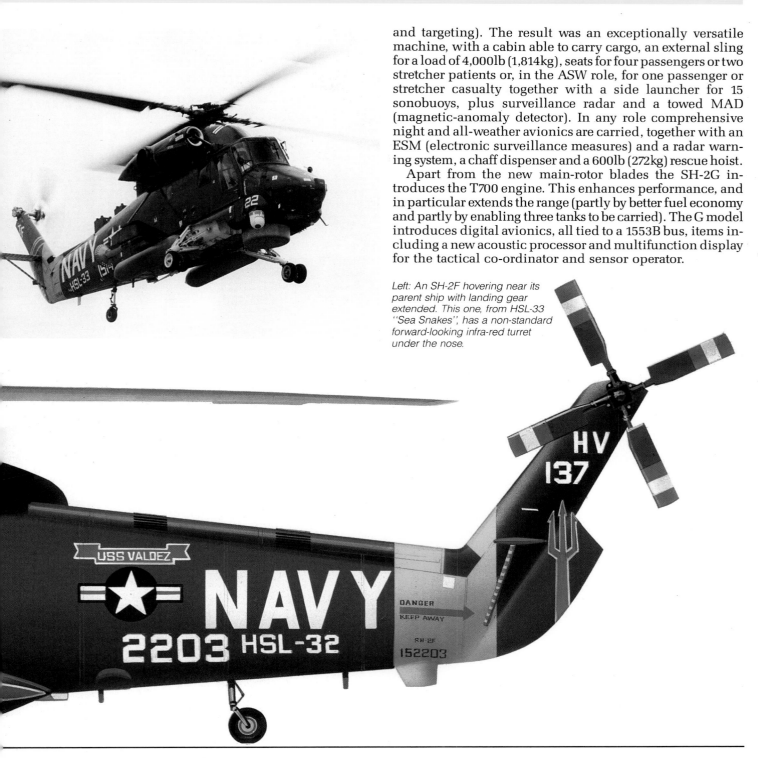

Left: An SH-2F hovering near its parent ship with landing gear extended. This one, from HSL-33 "Sea Snakes", has a non-standard forward-looking infra-red turret under the nose.

Kamov Ka-27, 28 and 29 "Helix"

Called "Helix" by NATO, this family of helicopters was developed by the design bureau named after its founder, Nikolai I. Kamov, to replace the same bureau's earlier Ka-25 (NATO "Hormone"). Like its predecessor, the Ka-27 is made particularly compact for operation from ships by its co-axial rotors. The twin engines are geared to concentric shafts which rotate in opposite directions, each shaft driving a three-blade rotor. The drive torques thus cancel out, so no tail rotor is needed. Instead an aeroplane-type tail is fitted, consisting

Origin: Soviet Union.
Engines: Two 2,225shp Isotov TV3-117V or 117VK.
Dimensions: Diameter of each main rotor (also overall length) 52ft 2in (15.9m).
Weights: Max slung load 11,023lb (5,000kg); max loaded (27B and 29) 26,455lb (12,000kg), (PS) 27,778lb (12,600kg).
Performance: Max speed (all) 165mph (265km/h); cruising speed (PS) 143mph (230km/h); range with full weapon load or max payload 115 miles (185km).
Armament: (27B) two 18in (450mm) ASW torpedoes, (29TB) four AT-6 "Spiral" missiles, or launchers for rockets of 2.24 or 3.15in (57 or 80mm) calibre (e.g. 80 of 80mm).
History: First flight (27 prototype) December 1974; first operational 1982.

of a fixed tailplane carrying elevators driven by the flight-control system for trimming purposes, as well as two large fins and rudders toed inwards at 25° and fitted with prominent leading-edge slats. The new main rotors have composite blades mounted in traditional articulated bearings in titanium hubs, and the leading edges are electrically de-iced whenever the engines are running.

Though mainly of aluminium alloy, the fuselage also incorporates titanium parts in highly stressed areas, and carries the tail on a tubular boom of composite material. The lower part of the fuselage is sealed to permit emergency water landings. The four units of the landing gear are basically fixed, though the levered-suspension nosewheels castor and in radar-equipped versions the main units can be raised out of the volume scanned by the radar antenna. Everything possi-

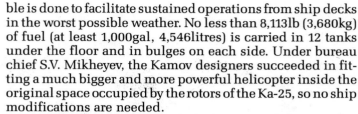

ble is done to facilitate sustained operations from ship decks in the worst possible weather. No less than 8,113lb (3,680kg) of fuel (at least 1,000gal, 4,546litres) is carried in 12 tanks under the floor and in bulges on each side. Under bureau chief S.V. Mikheyev, the Kamov designers succeeded in fitting a much bigger and more powerful helicopter inside the original space occupied by the rotors of the Ka-25, so no ship modifications are needed.

The AV-MF (Soviet naval aviation) operates three main versions. One is the Ka-27B for ASW missions, with 360° surveillance radar, doppler, provision for a box of sonobuoys, dipping sonar and towed MAD (magnetic-anomaly detection), and a prominent ESM (electronic surveillance measures) antenna above the rear fuselage. The Ka-27PS is an SAR (search and rescue) version, with radar, long-range tanks, comprehensive communications, a 660lb (300kg) rescue hoist with floodlight on the left side and a cabin which can be configured for 16 rescuees. The Ka-29TB is a Marines assault version with 12-14 armed troops, a data link and other sensors for guiding AT-6 missiles or friendly ships' cruise missiles. The Ka-28 is the export designation.

Western operators are regarding such machines as possible things to buy. With full avionics a Ka-27/32 is said to be priced at under $3 million.

Left: The profile shows a Ka-27 ASW helicopter of the Soviet AV-MF (Naval Aviation). The bulge under the rear fuselage houses doppler scan equipment, and the angular box further back houses twin gyrocompasses. No auxiliary tank is fitted, and the main wheels are fully deployed.

Below: The Ka-27PS is an SAR (search and rescue) helicopter, here again seen in AV-MF service. Its most obvious feature is the hydraulic hoist next to the main cabin door. Immediately ahead (on each side of the fuselage) are large, box-like fuel tanks which extend the "Helix's" range.

Kamov Ka-41 "Hokum"

It was in the summer of 1984 that Western defence analysts, presumably relying on satellite reconnaissance photographs, announced that the Soviet Union was flight-testing a completely new co-axial helicopter, which was given the NATO name of "Hokum". It remained a shadowy entity, illustrated only by a succession of progressively altered artist's impressions, until in 1989 the first photograph became available. How surprising, then, that when in May 1989 the deputy chief designer of the Kamov bureau, Venyamin Alekseyevich Kasjanikov, visited a helicopter meeting in the USA, he vehemently denied the existence of "Hokum", saying that his bureau designed naval helicopters exclusively. By the end of 1989 it was (supposedly) confirmed that "Hokum" is actually the Ka-41, but by this time Mr Kasjanikov had accompanied a Ka-32 (civil Ka-27) to Redhill, England, and again publicly denied that "Hokum" existed!

One can only conclude from this that, as this helicopter certainly does exist, it must be for use by the AV-MF, Soviet naval aviation. Previously it had been thought (by the US Defense Department, at least) to be a battlefield air vehicle.

Origin: Soviet Union.
Engines: Two 2,225shp Isotov TV3-117.
Dimensions: (Estimated) diameter of main rotors 45ft 10in (14.0m); overall length (rotors turning) 53ft 10in (16.4m).
Weights: Estimates of max loaded vary from 16,500 down to 12,500lb (7,500-5,450kg). Author estimates 22,000lb (10,000kg).
Performance: For several years the estimated maximum speed and combat radius have been, respectively, 217mph (350km/h) and 155 miles (250km).
Armament: Chin-mounted gun, almost certainly of 30mm calibre; the only photograph available shows, well outboard on the weapon wings, large rectangular boxes which (it has been surmised) might house the IR-guided version of the R-60 (AA-8 Aphid) close-range AAM, said to be carried by this helicopter. Many other weapons could be carried.
History: First flight, prior to 1984; operational capability, possibly 1990-91.

The DoD said in 1986, "It will give the Soviets a significant rotary-wing air-superiority capability. The system has no current Western counterpart." At first thought to be a rival to the Mi-28 in the anti-armour role, the Ka-41 has for at least three years been regarded as basically the world's first helicopter fighter aircraft, intended chiefly for shooting down other helicopters. Curiously, the co-axial rotors are widely

separated, whereas for high speed they need to have rigidly mounted blades quite close together. Indeed, the rotors look very like those of other Kamovs, except for the backswept tips to the blades. Another odd feature in a machine designed for speed is that the fuselage is wide enough to house the crew of two side-by-side.

The fuselage is at least well streamlined, ending in a large fin and rudder, with a tailplane (probably with elevators) well forward and carrying toed-in endplate fins. Tapered wings are mounted shoulder-high, with the engines mounted above the wing roots, requiring quite long shafts to drive the gearboxes to the rotors. The tailwheel landing gear is fully retractable, the main units folding into bulges along the lower sides of the fuselage. There are at least three and probably four weapon stations under each wing, though the plates on the tips appear to be for aerodynamic purposes only. The cockpit is certainly armoured, and the crew look through flat (probably bulletproof and non-glint) transparent panes. At the front are various sensors, including those for low and high airspeeds and probably a radar.

Right: In 1990 this was the only known photograph of the "Hokum", said to be the Kamov Ka-41, yet published. It shows the weapon wings carrying two large boxes (see comment on Armament in panel).

Below: A provisional drawing of what is believed to be the Ka-41, based on artwork issued by the US Dept of Defense. Note side-by-side cockpit, engine pods outside fuselage and the profusion of sensors.

MBB BO 105

Messerschmitt-Bölkow-Blohm, by far the biggest aerospace company in Germany, cannot have had any idea of the worldwide success they would achieve with the BO 105. Despite the fact that, according to one "expert" who viewed the prototype, "It is like other small helicopters but twice as expensive", by 1990 over 1,400 had been sold in 39 countries, and additional 105s were coming off the production lines in Germany, Spain, Indonesia and Canada.

All have basically the same airframe and dynamic parts, and all have the same twin turbine engines except for the Canadian 105 LS (lift and stretch) which has either uprated Allisons or the new Pratt & Whitney Canada PW205B, in 1990 flying in a prototype only. A key to the 105's renowned agility is the four-blade rotor, with glassfibre blades mounted rigidly (without hinges) into a forged titanium hub. The small engines are mounted close beneath the rotor hub on each side. At the front is the capacious cabin, with the pilot and either co-pilot or passenger at the front, and a bench seat at the rear for three, the latter being removable for loading cargo or two

Origin: West Germany.
Engines: Two 420shp Allison 250-C20B.
Dimensions: Diameter of main rotor 32ft 3.5in (9.84m); length overall (rotors turning) 38ft 11in (11.86m).
Weights: Empty (basic 105 CB) 2,813lb (1,276kg); normal loaded 5,291lb (2,400kg).
Performance: Max cruising speed 150mph (242km/h); hovering ceiling out of ground effect 5,300ft (1,615m); range at sea level, no reserve 357 miles (575km).
Armament: (PAH-1) six HOT wire-guided missiles, (Sweden) eight TOW.
History: First flight 16 February 1967; service delivery (VBH, PAH) both 1979.

stretcher casualties. There are two doors on each side and left/right clamshell doors at the back giving virtually unobstructed all-round access.

The biggest user of the BO 105 is the West German army, which by 1984 had received 100 BO 105M and 212 BO 105P helicopters, respectively with the military designations VBH and PAH-1. The VBH is an observation and liaison machine, and it is hoped from 1992 to convert 54 into BSH-1 interim fire-support and escort helicopters. The BSH-1 would have four Singer AAMs for self-defence or for engaging other air-

Above: The HOT missile tubes identify this BO 105 as a PAH-1 anti-armour helicopter serving with West Germany's Heèresflieger (Army aviation corps). Both the PAH-1 and its partner, the VBH, are being upgraded to improve their operational capabilities. The work is almost equivalent to building a new helicopter.

craft, and could later be equipped with night sights and other obviously needed equipment. Among various tests is one machine with a Lucas chin turret controlled by a Ferranti helmet-pointing sight for off-axis firing of Stinger missiles. The PAH-1 was expected to be an interim anti-tank helicopter until the Eurocopter Tiger could be available in about 1985, but it will now be the only helicopter available until after 1998. It was austerely equipped, having six HOT missiles and a SFIM APX397 roof sight, but no equipment for operating at night or in bad weather. Plans now exist to upgrade the PAH-1s in two phases, with C20R-3 engines, improved main-rotor blades, lighter weapon mounts and HOT 2 missiles with digital avionics. Loaded weight could increase to 5,511lb (2,500kg), enabling both crew members to be provided with a Leitz/Eltro/MBB night vision system.

Among many other users are the Swedish army with the HeliTOW system, the Spanish army with anti-tank or ground-attack weapons, and the Mexican navy with radar and flotation gear.

Left: A PAH-1 operating during an exercise in collaboration with friendly NATO ground forces. At present, the PAH-1 anti-armour missions are flown only in reasonable visual conditions, but even those operations can be a hazardous occupation at such low altitudes.

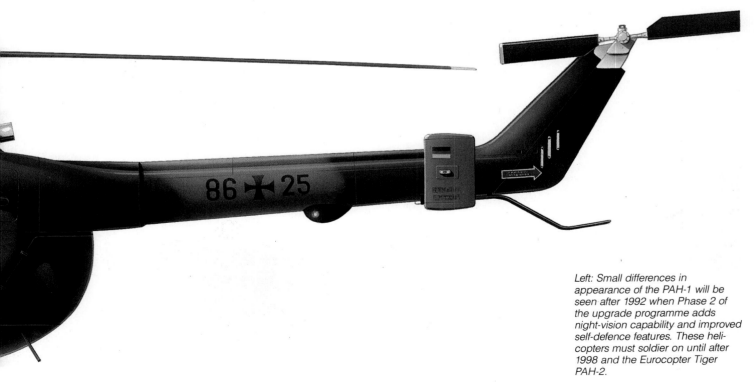

Left: Small differences in appearance of the PAH-1 will be seen after 1992 when Phase 2 of the upgrade programme adds night-vision capability and improved self-defence features. These helicopters must soldier on until after 1998 and the Eurocopter Tiger PAH-2.

McDonnell Douglas AH-64A Apache

Origin: USA.
Engines: Two 1,696shp General Electric T700-701.
Dimensions: Diameter of main rotor 48ft 0in (14.63m); length overall (rotors turning) 58ft 3.2in (17.76m).
Weights: Empty 10,760lb (4,881kg); max loaded 21,000lb (9,525kg).
Performance: Max level and max cruising speed 184mph (296km/h); hovering ceiling out of ground effect (at 14,445lb/6,552kg) 11,500ft (3,505m); max range (internal fuel) 300 miles (482km).
Armament: Up to 16 Hellfire missiles or four 19 × 2.75in rocket launchers; plus remotely aimed M230 Chain Gun of 30mm calibre.
History: First flight 30 September 1975; first delivery 26 January 1984.

Though it endured a long period of development, during which its appearance changed profoundly, once the AH-64A was perfected it has enjoyed a period of sustained high-rate manufacture which, unlike most programmes, results in deployment of powerful forces at minimum cost. At the same time, the AH-64A is a large and obtrusive machine, whose presence on the battlefield is obvious from many miles away; at present its sensors (excellent as they are) are in the nose, forcing the machine to expose itself, and it is inevitably expensive both to buy and to operate.

It won over its Bell rival in a 1975 competition for an AAH (advanced attack helicopter), to live with front-line troops, fight by night or in adverse weather (but not blind conditions) and survive hits by 12.7mm bullets (certain parts are intended to survive 23mm strikes). The engines are installed in giant armoured boxes, whose walls serve as working platforms and with enormous ejector nozzles through which issues the hot exhaust gas diluted by cool air to eliminate IR sources for heat-seeking missiles. The two drive shafts, which like other parts of the transmission are surrounded by armoured collars, turn

Left: Apaches are made at this completely new plant outside Mesa, Arizona. In ideal conditions, this facility has the advantage of building a product which has very little variation.

Below: A standard AH-64A, complete with ALQ-144 IR jammer on top. From 1993 up to 322 Apaches are to be completely upgraded in a multi-stage improvement programme.

the main gearbox and thence the rotor with four blades with backswept tips made mainly from steel and glassfibre. At the tail is a low all-moving tailplane and a tail rotor with pairs of blades set at the optimum 55°/125° angle for minimum noise.

The co-pilot-gunner sits in front with the pilot behind and 19in (480mm) higher, on seats designed to give 95 per cent survival even in a ground impact at 42ft (12.8m) per second. The windscreen is heated, an acrylic blast barrier separates the cockpits, and the floor and sides incorporate boron armour. Avionics are grouped in easily accessible boxes along the sides ahead of the fixed trailing arm main gears. In the nose are the integrated PNVS (pilot's night vision system), FLIR (forward-looking IR) and TADS (target acquisition and designation sight) comprising a second FLIR, a day TV camera with two magnifications, a laser spot tracker and a laser rangefinder/designator. Both crew wear IHADSS (integrated helmet and display sighting system) which displays flight data to the pilot, aiming cues for the CPG and other essential data on call.

So far prolonged efforts to get various forms of Sea-Going Apache into development have not borne fruit, but existing Apaches will certainly be upgraded in a multistage improvement programme. By early 1990 over 525 had been delivered, of a planned force which may very well be cut back from 975 to 807.

Above: A popular mixed armament is two quads of Hellfire missiles and two nineteen-tube rocket launchers. The large magazine behind the cockpits can house 1,200 rounds of 30mm.

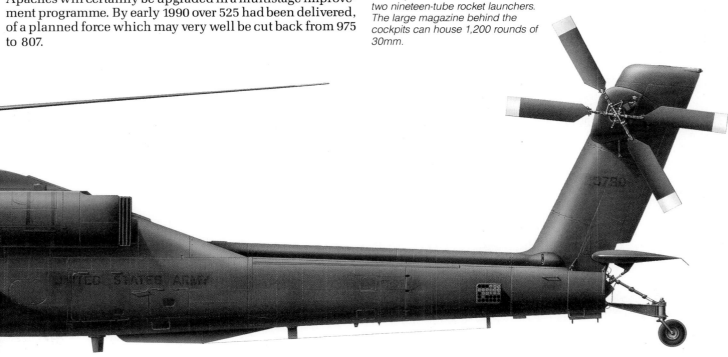

Mil Mi-8 ''Hip''

The design team of Mikhail L. Mil created the first helicopter to be built in quantity in the Soviet Union, in 1951. A little later came the Mi-4, which looked like a Sikorsky S-55 but actually had 1,700shp, and the Mi-6 of 1956 which represented the biggest quantum jump in the history of helicopters with 11,000shp and a weight of 93,700lb (42,500kg). In 1961 the Mi-8 prototype appeared, with a single engine. The production Mi-8 was twin-engined, and it has sustained the biggest production programme of any helicopter. Together with the more powerful Mi-17 it has been supplied to more than 40 air forces, and the total delivered is considerably in excess of 10,000. NATO name is ''Hip''.

This is all the more remarkable when it is remembered that this is a helicopter bigger than the Sea King, with a passenger capacity of up to 32. The airframe is of the classic pod-and-boom configuration, thus enabling vehicles or bulky freight to be loaded through clamshell doors at the rear. Most Mi-8s have been for military purposes, identified by having circular windows and, usually, various special communications, navigation and electronic-warfare equipment.

In all versions the twin engines are mounted close together

Origin: Soviet Union.
Engines: (8) two 1,700shp Isotov TV2-117A, (17A) two 1,900shp Isotov TV3-117MT, (17-1VA) two 2,225shp TV3-117VM.
Dimensions: Diameter of main rotor 69ft 10.2in (21.29m); length overall (rotors turning) (8) 82ft 9.7in (25.24m), (17) 83ft 2in (25.352m).
Weights: (Typical) empty (8) 16,007lb (7,260kg), (17) 15,653lb (7,100kg); max loaded (8) 26,455lb (12,000kg), (17) 28,660lb (13,000kg).
Performance: (At max weight) max cruising speed (8) 112mph (180km/h), (17) 149mph (240km/h); hovering ceiling out of ground effect at normal loaded weight (8) 2,625ft (800m), (17) 5,775ft (1,760m); range with standard fuel, both about 280 miles (450km).
Armament: The standard assault versions of both Mi-8 (MT and TBK) and Mi-17 have up to three stores attachments on each side, for example for a maximum of 192 rockets of 57mm calibre, or 120 of 80mm; 7.62mm PK machine guns can be fired through open side windows; some have a 12.7mm gun in the nose, aimed by the pilot not flying. Some Mi-17s have a fixed GSh-23L gun.
History: First flight early 1961 (with two engines and five-blade main rotor) 17 September 1962.

ahead of the rotor, with side jetpipes which can be screened to hide hot parts from hostile IR detectors or missiles. The Mi-8TBK, the standard front-line transport, also has 192 decoy flares. The main rotor has five blades of all-metal construction, carried in traditional articulated bearings and con-

trolled by irreversible hydraulic boosters. Fuel is carried in one internal tank and two drums hung on the outside, the right tank being smaller to allow for optional cabin-conditioning equipment to be installed in the front part of the fairing. Invariably the cockpit in the nose has dual controls, and many versions even carry a flight engineer. The tricycle landing gear is fixed, the twin nosewheels being steerable and the main wheels having pneumatic brakes. The Mi-17 has a gas-turbine APU (auxiliary power unit) behind the rotor, which among other things can provide compressed air for starting the main engines, and the Mi-17's inlets are protected by particle deflectors similar to those of later Mil helicopters.

Many Mi-8s and -17s, such as the 8M and 17MT, carry heavy armament for assault missions. Others are primarily transports, and there are many special versions, notably for communications relay, Elint (electronic intelligence), ECM and communications jamming and (Mi-17 displayed at the 1989 Paris show) a mobile surgical hospital.

Left: Mi-17 tactical helicopters of Soviet Frontal Aviation on exercise. Foreground machine is equipped to fire one hundred and ninety-two rockets and has a higher avionic standard than the Mi-8.

Below: The clamshell-type loading doors forming the rear of the Mi-8 fuselage pod allow easy access for both men and machinery. Up to thirty-two passengers can be accommodated.

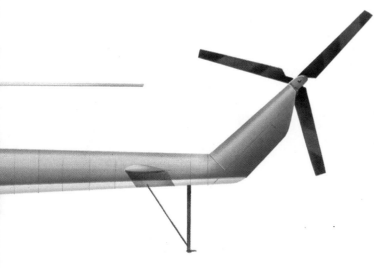

Left: Side elevation of typical mass-produced Mi-8TBK, showing ''Swatter'' anti-tank missiles (top),

57mm rocket launchers (below). Mi-8 and -17 tactical helicopters today have additional avionic items.

Mil Mi-14 ''Haze''

Origin: Soviet Union.
Engines: Two Isotov TV3, (early) 1,900shp TV3-117MT, (current) 2,300shp TV3-117VMA.
Dimensions: Diameter of main rotor 69ft 10.2in (21.29m); length overall (rotors turning) 83ft 2in (25.352m).
Weights: Empty (PL equipped) 16,534lb (7,500kg); max loaded 30,865lb (14,000kg).
Performance: Max speed 143mph (230km/h); max cruising speed 124mph (200km/h); range with max fuel (presumably no weapon load) 705 miles (1,135km).
Armament: (PL) central bay along bottom, with twin hinged doors, for maximum of four 18in (457mm) AS torpedoes, or various types of depth charge or mine; (BT, PS) usually none.
History: First flight (V-14) September 1969.

Developed from the original Mi-8 in parallel with the Mi-17, and using the Mi-17 engines, transmission and rotors, the Mi-14 was produced to meet a need for an amphibious helicopter for various overwater missions. The lower part of the fuselage is completely redesigned to incorporate a flying-boat type sealed bottom. Unlike other watertight helicopters the Mi-14 is specifically designed for sustained amphibious operations, though of course not in severe sea states. For stability on the water large sponsons, with strakes and flotation bags, are fitted on each side at the rear of the main part of the fuselage, and a small float mounted on struts beneath the tail keeps the tail rotor clear of the water. For land and ship operations a quadricycle landing gear is fitted, all four units retracting fully. The castoring and optionally steerable nose units each have a single lever-suspended wheel, are similar to those of the Mi-8 and retract forwards into open boxes in the hull. The main gears have twin wheels and retract backwards into the sponsons, which also house fuel (external drums being removed).

As the V-14 the prototypes of this helicopter required a large development programme. They were the first to be powered by the TV3 engine, which not only provides more power but is smaller and results in a visibly different installation. Surprisingly, all Mi-14s so far seen have plain engine inlets, with no baffles, filter boxes or ice protection, and with plain jet-pipes without IR protection. Other new items were a new gearbox, larger power-driven stabilizer (tailplane) and a modified tail rotor moved from the right side to the left.

The first variant put into production, in 1976, was the

Mi-14PL. This, called "Haze-A", by NATO, is an ASW machine equipped very fully with ASW sensors and weapons and with a crew of five, comprising two pilots in a cockpit very similar to the Mi-17, and three sensor operators (one being the tactical commander) in the main tactical compartment. Like all variants the PL has a 360° search radar under the nose. Other sensors include a towed MAD (magnetic-anomaly detection) receiver towed from a winch at the rear and groups of sonobuoys.

The Mi-14BT is an MCM (mine countermeasures) version, with the same comprehensive ESM/EW receivers as the PL (but of course no ASW gear), extra avionics (some on each side of the doppler box under the tail boom) and a long cable fairing and large pod (with ram inlet) on the right side, in addition to the minesweeping gear. The Mi-14PS is an SAR (search and rescue) model, with a hoist, wide sliding door, twin searchlights and the strake and pod of the BT. Mi-14s have been exported to at least seven countries.

Below: The Mi-14PL "Haze-A" is the basic ASW version of this twin-engined Soviet helicopter. From the side it is not possible to see the long weapons bay along the centreline, nor the various sensors recessed into the lower rear fuselage. However, the MAD "bird" can be seen stowed against the rear of the fuselage pod, and the port-side flotation bag and the inflatable tail float are visible.

Above: The Mi-14 can undertake conventional landings as well as amphibious operations, thanks to its quadricycle landing gear. All four units can be fully retracted, with the main units being sponson-housed.

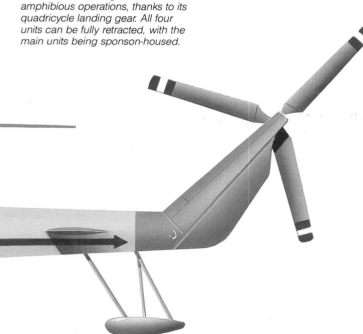

Mil Mi-24, 25 and 35 "Hind"

Origin: Soviet Union.
Engines: All current versions, two 2,200shp Isotov TV3-117M.
Dimensions: Diameter of main rotor 56ft 9in (17.3m); length overall (rotors turning) 71ft 6.3in (21.8m).
Weights: (Mi-24P) empty equipped 18,078lb (8,200kg); normal loaded 24,692lb (11,200kg), max loaded 26,455lb (12,000kg).
Performance: Max speed 208mph (335km/h); cruising speed 168mph (270km/h); hovering ceiling out of ground effect 4,921ft (1,500m); range (internal fuel, 5 per cent reserve) 280 miles (450km).
Armament: (Most) six wing pylons for (typically) two pairs of AT-6 Spiral on tips and four launchers for 57, 80, 130 or 240mm rockets on the inners; (24, 25) remotely sighted chin turret for four-barrel 12.7mm gun, (24P, 35P) single GSh-30-2 twin-barrel 30mm cannon fixed to fire ahead.
History: First flight 1970, first delivery 1973.

By far the most widely used armed attack helicopter in the world, this familiar family, called "Hind" by NATO, was the last creation of Mikhail Mil himself. He pushed it through, often against official opposition, during the 1960s. To save costs (because this was largely a private development), the helicopter was based on the Mi-8, but of course the main part of the fuselage had to be new. In the event a new rotor was adopted, with shorter blades stressed for higher g-loads and with aluminium largely replaced by steel and titanium as part of the policy of surviving 20mm strikes. Later the TV2 engine was replaced by the TV3, the tail rotor was moved to the left and the blades were redesigned with an extruded titanium spar and glassfibre skin.

Unlike other helicopters the fuselage combined an attack front end, with a weapon-system officer in the nose and the pilot above and behind, with a main cabin seating eight equipped troops. Fuel is under the floor. High on each side are downward-sloping weapon wings. Engine inlets in most versions are fitted with deflector baffles for dust and sand,

while most models have upturned and shrouded jetpipes to reduce IR signature. The tricycle landing gear is retractable, though in all except early models the steerable twin-wheel nose unit does not retract fully. The single-wheel main gears fold inwards to the rear, the doors incorporating large bulges.

Early versions had a three-seat cockpit with flat transparent panels and a hand-aimed gun, but these were quickly superseded by today's versions. These have the tandem seats, with full dual controls and a moving-map display in each cockpit, the pilot having steps to a side door and the WSO

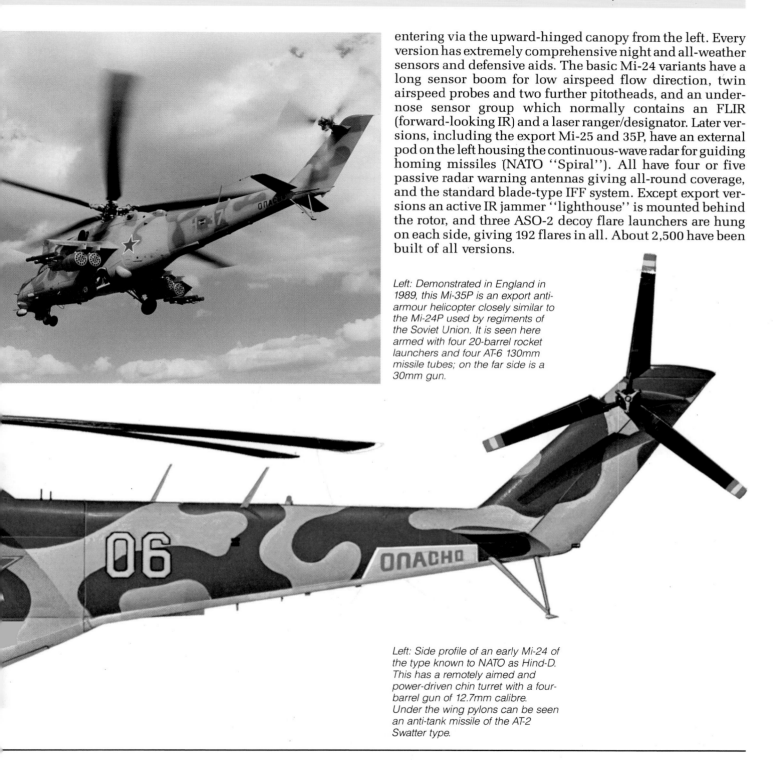

entering via the upward-hinged canopy from the left. Every version has extremely comprehensive night and all-weather sensors and defensive aids. The basic Mi-24 variants have a long sensor boom for low airspeed flow direction, twin airspeed probes and two further pitotheads, and an under-nose sensor group which normally contains an FLIR (forward-looking IR) and a laser ranger/designator. Later versions, including the export Mi-25 and 35P, have an external pod on the left housing the continuous-wave radar for guiding homing missiles (NATO "Spiral"). All have four or five passive radar warning antennas giving all-round coverage, and the standard blade-type IFF system. Except export versions an active IR jammer "lighthouse" is mounted behind the rotor, and three ASO-2 decoy flare launchers are hung on each side, giving 192 flares in all. About 2,500 have been built of all versions.

Left: Demonstrated in England in 1989, this Mi-35P is an export anti-armour helicopter closely similar to the Mi-24P used by regiments of the Soviet Union. It is seen here armed with four 20-barrel rocket launchers and four AT-6 130mm missile tubes; on the far side is a 30mm gun.

Left: Side profile of an early Mi-24 of the type known to NATO as Hind-D. This has a remotely aimed and power-driven chin turret with a four-barrel gun of 12.7mm calibre. Under the wing pylons can be seen an anti-tank missile of the AT-2 Swatter type.

Mil Mi-26 ''Halo''

Origin: Soviet Union.
Engines: Two 11,240shp Lotarev D-136.
Dimensions: Diameter of main rotor 105ft 0in (32.0m); length overall (rotors turning) 131ft 3.8in (40.025m).
Weights: Empty 62,170lb (28,200kg); normal loaded 109,125lb (49,500kg); max loaded 123,459lb (56,000kg).
Performance: Max speed 183mph (259km/h); cruising speed 158mph (255km/h); hovering ceiling out of ground effect 5,906ft (1,800m); range, internal fuel and 5 per cent reserve 497 miles (800km).
Armament: Not normally fitted.
History: First flight 14 December 1977; service delivery 1983.

Having created in the Mi-6 by far the biggest and most powerful helicopter in the world, the design bureau of Mikhail Mil next tried to build a machine with exactly twice the capability. They did this in the 1960s with the V-12, which had a gigantic central fuselage and, far out on each side, an Mi-6 powerplant group and rotor. The V-12 (Mi-12) was not really a success, and after Mil's death in 1970 the new team, led by Marat Tishchyenko, started again. This time they accepted the need to start from scratch, and the engine bureau of V.A. Lotarev (today the ZMKB) developed the very powerful new engine. Wisely, it was decided to stick to the traditional formula of one main and one tail rotor.

It is a measure of the advance in helicopter technology that the resulting Mi-26 has more than double the installed power of the Mi-6, yet its main rotor is actually smaller. One explanation is that the number of blades has gone up to eight, and of course the aerodynamic profiles are much better. At the same time, partly because operations in remote Siberia (for example) demand absolute reliability, the blades retain spars of high-tensile steel tube, though the rest of the blade is Nomex honeycomb with a glassfibre skin. The hub is a huge titanium-alloy forging, with the blades held in articulated hinges with duplicated hydraulic jacks for each (collective and cyclic) channel, plus stability-augmentation and autopilot inputs. The five blades of the tail rotor are glassfibre, and all blades have electric de-icing.

The engines drive through the most impressive gearbox ever made for an aircraft, much less than half the weight of that of the Mi-6 despite transmitting twice the power. Engine inlets have vortex-type sand/dust separators, and the cowl panels form work platforms, with access via a roof hatch or steps up the fuselage side. Above and between the engines

Left: So far as is known, the only export customer for the mighty Mi-26 so far has been the Indian Air Force, which is so pleased with its first ten (delivered from June 1986) that it wishes to buy more. Certainly no other helicopter comes near the big Mil in transport capability. Western certification is being sought, and the type is said to be priced at about US$28 million with spares. In the spirit of glasnost, Western companies are being offered the chance to lease Halos.

is a large fan-assisted oil cooler, looking like a third engine. The actual third engine (the APU, auxiliary power unit) is under the flight deck. No less than 2,640gal of fuel is housed under the floor.

The pressurized flight deck seats a crew of five. Equipment includes weather radar, doppler, autopilot with autohover mode, TV for watching slung loads and, in military versions such as the 26VT, chaff/flare dispensers and IR jammers. Typical loads include 85 equipped troops, or cargo up to 44,090lb (20,000kg). About 300 Mi-26T and VT helicopters have been built. NATO calls them ''Halo''.

Left: This side profile shows one of the Mi-26 heavy lift helicopters built in 1990 for Soviet military use, which has accounted for about half of the total of 330. Current (1990) production Mi-26s have uprated engines, glassfibre composite blades and other upgrades, the payload going up to 48,500lb (22 tonnes). The civil designation of the original version of the ''Halo'' is Mi-26T.

Mil Mi-28 "Havoc"

Origin: Soviet Union.
Engines: Two 2,200shp Isotov TV3-117M.
Dimensions: Diameter of main rotor 56ft 5.2in (17.2m); length overall (rotors turning) 70ft 5in (21.49m).
Weights: Empty (equipped) 14,330lb (6,500kg); max loaded 25,133lb (11,400kg).
Performance: Max speed (also max cruising speed) at max weight 186mph (300km/h); hovering ceiling out of ground effect 11,811ft (3,600m); range with max weapons 298 miles (480km).
Armament: One 30mm 2A42 high-velocity gun (operator can select HE or AP feed at any time); 5,290lb (2,400kg) of wing-mounted rockets (inboard 20 × 57 or 70mm) and missiles (outboard 16 AT-6 Spiral).
History: First flight 10 November 1982; service delivery, late 1991.

Despite the fact that it is a derivative of the Mi-24, this dedicated attack helicopter has had a very long gestation, and it will be over nine years between the first flight and first delivery for service. Various mostly minor problems have been experienced, but the main cause of delay has been the inability of the various sensors to be qualified for inclusion.

Called "Havoc" by NATO, the Mi-28 has a main rotor slightly smaller than that of the Mi-24, but it differs completely in design. The forged titanium hub holds the five blades in elastomeric attachments, eliminating all bearings, and the blades have filament-wound glassfibre D-spars, Nomex trailing edge and composite skin. At the diagonally cropped tip is a low-airspeed sensor and tracking mass box. The tail rotor, moved to the right side, may have three or four blades (examples of both are on test). The fuselage, mainly of metal, is totally new and enables the rotor mast and gearbox to be sunk into the space occupied by the cabin in the Mi-24. The engines are thus installed wide apart on each side of the fuselage, which in turn enables the cockpits to be close up in front of the rotor hub. The weapon wings sit on the fuselage proper under the rear of the gearbox, and the engines are mounted on the same structure.

Each engine has a vortex-type particle separator ahead of the inlet. At the other end the Nos 1 and 2 prototypes have straight jetpipes with overhead inlets to a huge IR suppressing box, whereas No 3 has downturned jetpipes with cooling inlets facing ahead on the outer side of the engine. Electronic engine control sustains full power to 6,561ft (2,000m). A gas-turbine APU (auxiliary power unit) is installed aft of the rotor, mainly to provide ground power. Fuel is housed in centre-fuselage tanks protected by thick composite armour. Unlike the Mi-24 the weapons operator in the front cockpit does not (in existing prototypes, at least) have full dual flight controls. He has basic flight instruments and a large two-handed controller for the sensors and gun, which it is intended to link with a helmet sight system. In front is

a large vizor-equipped sensor display. When available the sensor kit will comprise a multimode radar, a large turret housing magnifying optics and a laser ranger/designator, a fixed FLIR (forward-looking IR) on the left and an LLTV (low-light TV) on the right. The crew board through side doors, the pilot high on the right and the WO on the left. Heavy titanium armour and 2in (50mm) glass protects both cockpits.

Left: A close-up view of the Mi-28 port jetpipe illustrates the down-turned configuration adopted on the third ''Havoc'' prototype, as seen at the Paris Air Show in 1989 (the first and second prototypes had upturned jetpipes). The prominent grill intake at the front of the unit provides copious amounts of cooling air to help reduce the exhaust gas heat signature.

Below: The hard-learnt lessons of the war in Afghanistan have been incorporated in the fearsome Mi-28 ''Havoc'' anti-tank helicopter — the Soviet answer to the US Army's AH-64A Apache. Like its American counterpart, the Mi-28 sports a chin-mounted high-velocity gun, and rockets or missile packs carried on weapon wings mounted under the engine gearbox.

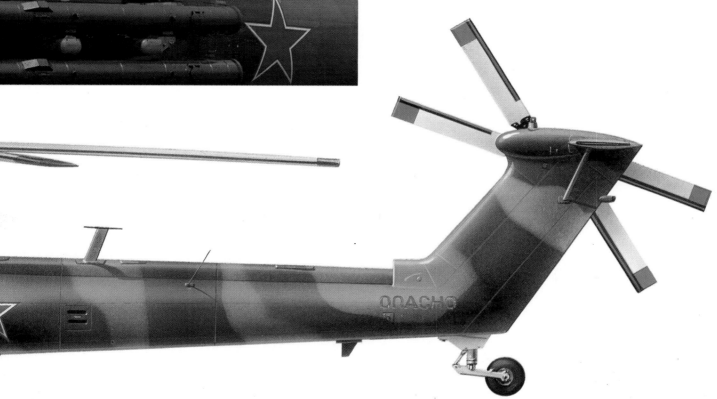

Sikorsky S-61

Origin: USA.
Engines: Two General Electric T58, (SH-3H) 1,400shp T58-10, (AS-61 versions) 1,500shp T58-100.
Dimensions: Diameter of main rotor 62ft 0in (18.9m); length overall (rotors turning) (most) 71ft 10.7in (21.91m), (R versions) 73ft 0in (22.25m).
Weights: Empty (bare S-61A) 9,763lb (4,428kg), (R) 13,255lb (6,010kg); max loaded (S-61A) 21,500lb (9,750kg), (R) 22,050lb (10,000kg).
Performance: Cruising speed (all) 136-144mph (219-232km/h); hovering ceiling out of ground effect (typical, 20,500lb 9,300kg) 8,200ft (2,500m); range (ASH-3H, 31 troops) 362 miles (582km); (R) can fly 276 miles (445km), pick up 24 troops and return with full fuel reserve.
Armament: (SH-3H) 840lb (380kg) of weapons; (ASH-3H up to four A 244AS, Mk 44 or Mk 46 torpedoes.
History: First flight 11 March 1959, (R) 17 June 1963.

Above: The S-61 Sea King first introduced the concept of the amphibious helicopter with retractable landing gear, as well as safety of twin gas-turbine engines.

Developed as the HSS-2 helicopter of the US Navy, later (1962) redesignated as the SH-3 and named Sea King, the S-61 was a landmark in helicopter technology. Virtually an Mi-6 on a much smaller scale, it was the first really successful turbine helicopter to go into production in the West, apart from

the small Alouette. It also introduced the concept of having an amphibious capability, with a boat-type hull, and the ASW versions were the first ever successfully to have the capability of undertaking both the search and the attack functions. Previously the ASW mission had required two helicopters, one carrying the sensors and the other the weapons.

In contrast to piston-engined Sikorskys, the S-61 has the engines above the fuselage, enabling the flight crew of two or three to be in the nose. The main cabin has room for up to 31 troops or other passengers, and up to 6,000lb (2,721kg) of cargo can be carried internally or 8,000lb (3,630kg) on a sling. In the ASW role the cabin is a tactical compartment where three operators co-ordinate the inputs from a search radar under the fuselage, a towed MAD (magnetic-anomaly detection) receiver, active and passive sonobuoys and ESM (electronic surveillance measures). Most ASW versions also carry sonar, dipped in the ocean on a cable from a winch.

The original, and most numerous, S-61 airframe has tailwheel landing gear with twin-wheel main units retrac-

ting backwards into the stabilizing floats. The crew door is on the left, and the cabin has a large sliding door on the right. As a private venture Sikorsky also developed the S-61R, configured as a transport. This has a different rear fuselage with a full-width rear ramp and door for loading bulky cargo or vehicles, the tail rotor being carried on a slim boom, fin and high half tailplane. The landing gear was redesigned, with semi-retractable twin nosewheels and twin mainwheels retracting forwards into large sponsons which permit amphibious operation, even with the rear door open. Both configurations are used in the SAR (search and rescue) role, with a 600lb (272kg) hoist and accommodation for 15 stretcher casualties and one or two attendants. Various HH-3 "Jolly Green" armed rescue versions were used in Vietnam with guns, armour, a flight-refuelling probe and drop tanks.

Sikorsky built nearly 800 of all versions, and a further 400 were added by licensees Westland (see separate entry), Mitsubishi and Agusta. The two latter companies expected to complete manufacture of new S-61s in 1990.

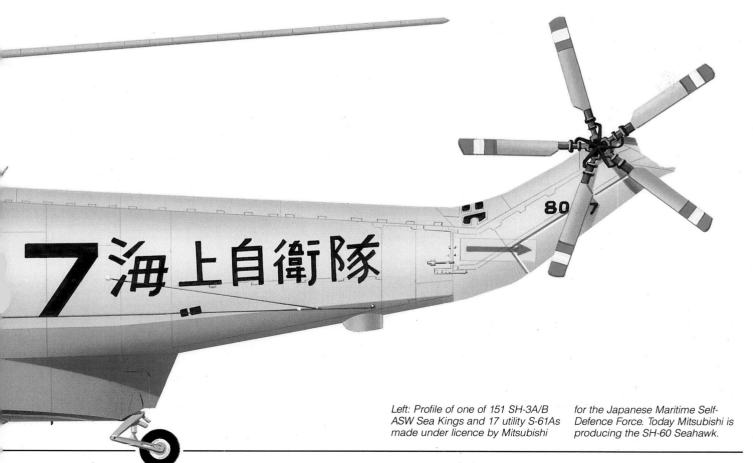

Left: Profile of one of 151 SH-3A/B ASW Sea Kings and 17 utility S-61As made under licence by Mitsubishi for the Japanese Maritime Self-Defence Force. Today Mitsubishi is producing the SH-60 Seahawk.

Sikorsky S-65

Origin: USA.
Engines: (Prior to E) two General Electric T64 rated at 2,850, 3,080, 3,925 or 4,380shp; (E) three 4,380shp T64-416.
Dimensions: Diameter of main rotor (pre-E) 72ft 3in (22.02m), (E) 79ft 0in (24.08m); length overall (rotors turning) (pre-E) 88ft 3in (26.9m), (E) 99ft 0.5in (30.19m).
Weights: Empty (CH-53A) 23,505lb (10,662kg), (CH-53E) 33,228lb (15,072kg); max loaded (CH-53A) 39,760lb (15,875kg), (CH-53E, slung load) 73,500lb (33,340kg).
Performance: Maximum speed (all) 196mph (315km/h); cruising speed (E) 173mph (278km/h); hovering ceiling out of ground effect (E) 9,500ft (2,895m).
Armament: Not normally carried, but provision is made for various (as yet unspecified) weapons in MH-53J.
History: First flight 14 October 1964, (E) 1 March 1974.

This family includes some of the most powerful helicopters outside the Soviet Union. Starting 30 years ago with a requirement for a heavy assault transport helicopter for the US Marine Corps, the S-65 series entered production as the CH-53A Stallion with two engines of 2,850shp and is today still in production as the Super Stallion and Sea Dragon with three engines of 4,380shp each! Few helicopters can come anywhere near this power upgrade of 130 per cent.

The original CH-53A had a configuration similar to that of the S-61R (which it preceded). The unobstructed cabin, 90in (2.29m) wide and 78in (1.98m) high, ends in a full-section rear ramp door for loading bulky cargo, light vehicles or other cargo up to 12,000lb (5,443kg). Up to 20,000lb (9,072kg) could be carried as a slung load for short distances. Maximum seating was for 38 troops. Apart from the greater size the CH-53A differed from the S-61R (CH-3) in having a normal fuselage with no boat-type bottom (though it is sealed for emergency water landings), a main rotor with six instead of five blades and engines mounted far apart in nacelles outboard of the fuselage. Sikorsky delivered 139 CH-53As, 15 of which were fitted with 3,925shp engines and converted into RH-53A MCM (mine countermeasures) sweeping helicopters for the US Navy.

In 1966 the US Air Force began ordering a succession of progressively upgraded HH-53 "Super Jolly" long-range rescue transports for Vietnam. These had drop tanks, a retractable flight-refuelling probe, hoist, special navaids, armour

Below: The CH-53E is unusual in being a slightly asymmetric aircraft with two of its three engines to left of the centreline. Another odd feature, not seen here, is that the entire tail leans over to the left. Later Super Stallions have modified tail, with a narrower fin.

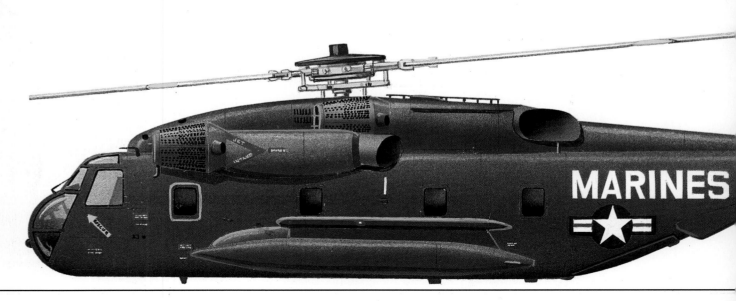

and much extra equipment including three 7.62mm Miniguns, 20mm cannon or other weapons. But by far the biggest upgrade was triggered by a 1972 Marines need for a helicopter to lift 16 US tons over short distances. After political delays this superb machine, the CH-53E Super Stallion, reached the Marines in June 1981. Among other things it has a third engine, main rotor with seven blades with titanium spars, Nomex cores and glassfibre skins, a substantially redesigned fuselage with considerable composite construction, much greater fuel capacity, and a digital flight-control system. Seating capacity is increased to 55 troops, and external payload limit is 36,000lb (16,330kg).

Two further important families have stemmed from the CH-53E. Appreciable numbers (31 by late 1989) have been produced of the MH-53E Sea Dragon for the Navy, replacing the RH-53A in MCM duties. The most obvious change is the enormous sponson on each side, giving fuel capacity of 2,664gal (12,113litres). The MH-53J "Pave Low Enhanced" is an assault transport for the Special Operations Forces, equipped for long missions by night or in adverse weather.

Despite the great cost of these machines, an export market is now opening up. Japan is first, with a requirement for twelve.

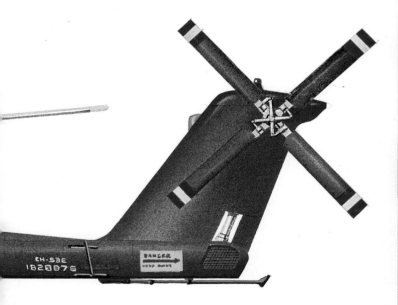

Above: Some extremely successful trials were held with the first MH-53E Sea Dragon in 1983 and between 1986 and 1988 Sikorsky was required to cease production of CH-53Es in order to concentrate entirely on mine-countermeasures (MCM) version.

Sikorsky S-70A

Origin: USA.
Engines: Two General Electric T700, (most) 1,560shp T700-700, (MH-60K and export models) 1,723shp T700-701A.
Dimensions: Diameter of main rotor 53ft 8in (16.36m); length overall (rotors turning) 64ft 10in (19.76m).
Weights: Empty (UH) 11,284lb (5,118kg); max loaded 22,000lb (9,979kg).
Performance: (UH, at 16,994lb/7,708kg) max cruising speed 167mph (268km/h); hovering ceiling out of ground effect 10,400ft (3,170m); range with max internal fuel (implying payload of 2,710lb/1,229kg) 373 miles (600km).
Armament: Usually none, but two lateral pintle mounts can take a 7.62mm Minigun or 0.5in/12.7mm Gecal 50; ESSS can carry (normally for transport only) 16 Hellfires or M56 mine dispensing pods; (MH-60A) door-mounted Minigun; (MH-60K) two door-mounted Gecal 50 and provision for Stinger AAMs.
History: First flight 17 October 1974, (EH) 24 September 1981, (MH-60K) 1990.

This extremely successful programme began with Sikorsky's win over a Boeing rival in 1976 of what the US Army called the UTTAS (utility tactical transport aircraft system). The result so far has been production of 1,200 UH-60A Black Hawks, of a planned requirement for 2,253. Features of this helicopter include two specially developed engines offering good fuel economy and high reliability in tough front-line conditions, a main rotor with four composite blades held in elastomeric (bearingless) mounts in a forged titanium hub, a fuselage which in plan looks to be of the pod-and-boom type but from the side appears streamlined, a fixed tailwheel type landing gear which places the cabin level and close to the ground, and a large tailplane powered through up to ±34° by dual electric actuators according to airspeed, pitch attitude rate, collective position and lateral acceleration.

The cockpit has dual controls, and there is a gunner's position for a third crew-member in the cabin. The latter has a large sliding door on each side. Loads can include 11 equipped troops (high-density option, 14), six stretcher patients and attendants, or a 105mm howitzer and its crew of five and 50 rounds, the last load requiring the external hook rated at 8,000lb (3,629kg). An important addition from UH-60 No 431 onwards is the ESSS (external stores support system), which adds four pylons from which loads up to a total of more than 10,000lb (4,536kg) can be hung. Loads can include weapons (see data), ECM packs, motorcycles or four tanks giving an unrefuelled range of 1,380 miles (2,220km).

Sikorsky delivered 66 EH-60A electronic-warfare helicopters, used by the US Army to intercept, locate, monitor and jam hostile communications as an element of the SEMA (special electronics mission aircraft) programme. The EH-60A has a rear fuselage bristling with dipole and whip antennas and other additions. Nine VH-60As are VIP transports, with special avionics and other equipment, for the Marine Corps Executive Flight Detachment. The USAF and Air National Guard fly 20 MH-60G Pave Hawk rescue helicopters. These have extra all-weather navaids and communications, additional fuel, a retractable flight refuelling probe and provision for guns (see data). In 1990 Sikorsky was expecting to build 60 MH-60K Army SOAs (special operations aircraft), to follow 30 simpler MH-30As. These will have exceptionally complete avionics for nap-of-the-Earth flight at night or in adverse weather, including terrain following/terrain avoidance radar, a forward-looking IR, FR probe, hoist, folding tailplane, external tanks and various weapons.

Left: Few helicopters have had their performance and utility (not to mention fighting ability) so transformed as the UH-60A when fitted with the ESSS. As explained in the text, this enables a very wide range of loads, including weapons, to be carried externally. In this case, the loads comprise two different types of rocket launcher and two 0.5in gun pods, enabling the UH-60A to carry out a variety of ground support operations.

Below: This photograph shows that, even with ESSS loads, the UH-60A can still carry internal and external loads, though the normal mission gross weight is 16,994lb (7,708kg), the figure in the data being ''alternative'' overload. Sikorsky hopes to replace the UH-60A in production in 1992 with an uprated model, the UH-60M. This would have a new swept-tip rotor of composite material, longer fuselage, uprated engines as well as other changes and an enhanced overall operational capability.

Below: Side profile of an early production UH-60A operating with the US Army in the casevac role. Like the very much cheaper Bell UH-1H, the UH-60A accommodates six stretcher (litter) casualties, but it offers both a faster and smoother ride.

Sikorsky S-70B

> **Origin:** USA.
> **Engines:** Two General Electric T700, (pre-1988) 1,690shp T700-401, (since 1988) 1,900shp T700-401C.
> **Dimensions:** As UH-60A, except, length with rotors and tail folded reduced by 5in (127mm) to 40ft 11in (12.47m).
> **Weights:** (SH-60B, ASW mission) empty 13,648lb (6,191kg); max loaded 20,244lb (9,182kg).
> **Performance:** Not stated, except dash speed (short-time max) 145mph (234km/h).
> **Armament:** (ASW) two Mk 46 torpedoes, (ASST) two Penguin Mk 2 Mod 7 anti-ship missiles, (HH) two pintle-mounted M60D 7.62mm machine guns.
> **History:** First flight 12 December 1979, (HH) 17 August 1988.

The concept of the LAMPS having been established with the Kaman SH-2 Seasprite (see above), the US Navy developed the concept via the stillborn LAMPS II to LAMPS III. This defined the requirements for a more advanced shipboard helicopter able to fly both ASW and ASST (anti-ship surveillance and targeting) missions. The prime contract was won in 1974 by IBM, which then had to select a suitable helicopter. The choice fell on a derivative of the UH-60, and this has since been delivered in quantity to the US Navy as the SH-60B Seahawk. This is being deployed aboard 95 surface warships, 260 being required.

Apart from the paint scheme the only obvious changes are the twin-wheel tail gear, moved forward and with a long extending leg, the surveillance radar under the cockpit, the four passive ECM receiver boxes on each side of the nose and rear fuselage, and the launcher for 25 sonobuoys on the left side. Less obvious are more powerful engines, removal of armour, folding tail and auto-folding main rotor with brake, rescue hoist, larger untapered tailplane, sliding cockpit door, greater fuel capacity (and provision for tanks on the added weapon pylons, and a hover-in-flight refuelling system to take fuel from ships), buoyancy features and an RAST (recovery assist, secure and traversing) to facilitate landing on small decks in rough weather and subsequent movement into a hangar.

The SH-60B naturally has extremely comprehensive avionics for searching for submarines by night or in adverse weather. The radar, whose antenna rotates inside a large but shallow radome, is the Texas Instruments APS-124. The same company supplies the ASQ-81 MAD (magnetic-anomaly detection) receiver which is normally parked on a pylon projecting from the right of the rear fuselage. Normally the crew comprises a pilot and an airborne tactical officer or backup pilot in the cockpit and a single sensor operator in the cabin. The ESM system is the Raytheon ALQ-142. Basically similar

helicopters are the S-70B-2 for the Royal Australian Navy, which has MEL Super Searcher radar and Collins integrated avionics, and the SH-60J which will be licence-built by Mitsubishi for Japan.

In 1989 Sikorsky began delivering the SH-60F Ocean Hawk. Long studied as the CV-Helo, this will operate from US Navy carriers to protect the inner zone of a carrier battle group against submarine attack. Its main feature is the Allied Signal (Bendix) AQS-13F dipping sonar, which replaces the sonobuoy launcher and all other SH-60B sensors. Other sensors and avionics may be installed later to support SAR (search and rescue), plane-guard and anti-ship attack. A total of 175 are required. The Navy has also received 18 HH-60H strike/rescue/special warfare support helicopters. These operate from warships or unprepared sites, and have comprehensive radar and IR warning and jamming, screened jetpipes, night-vision goggles and guns.

Though not strictly combat machines, the 15 HH-60J Jayhawk helicopters of the US Coast Guard will be armed with M-60D machine guns and have comprehensive avionics.

Below: From left side the 25-tube sonobuoy launcher is prominent, as are the large but shallow radome under the cockpit and the rectangular box ESM antennas on nose and amidships.

Right: One of the first Seahawks to enter service, seen in this picture with its parent ship, the frigate USS Crommelin. The Seahawk is a large machine, and requires a substantial deck area.

Westland Sea King

Origin: UK (licence from USA).
Engines: (Current models) two 1,660shp Rolls-Royce Gnome H.1400-1T.
Dimensions: Diameter of main rotor 62ft 0in (18.9m); length overall (rotors turning) 72ft 8in (22.15m).
Weights: Empty 11,891lb (5,393kg), (equipped for ASW) 16,377lb (7,428kg); max loaded 21,500lb (9,752kg).
Performance: Cruising speed 126mph (204km/h); hovering ceiling out of ground effect 4,700ft (1,433m); range (max standard fuel) 921 miles (1,482km).
Armament: (ASW) four Sting Ray, Mk 46 or A 244S torpedoes, or Mk 11 depth charges or one Clevite simulator, (ASSV) two Sea Eagle or AM 39 Exocet, (Commando) very wide range of customer options for guns, rockets and missiles.
History: First flight (HAS.1) 7 May 1969, (Commando) 12 September 1973.

Westland obtained a licence to build the Sikorsky S-61 in 1959. Since then the same basic helicopter has been made in numerous versions, all differing from the original. The first, to meet the obvious Royal Navy need for a modern ASW helicopter, was the HAS.1, based on the SH-3D (but with British engines and avionics). The crucial difference was that the HAS.1 had to carry out independent ASW search and attack missions without any link to the parent ship. Thus, equipment included Ekco search radar with a dorsal antenna, doppler, autopilot (with autotransition to the hover) and dunking (dipping) sonar. A large number of derived helicopters were supplied to many export customers, for ASW, anti-ship attack and, especially, SAR (search and rescue).

The HAS.2, to which surviving Mk 1s were converted, plus 21 built as such, has uprated engines and transmission, a sixth tail-rotor blade, stronger airframe and better fuel jettison. The AEW.2A is an airborne early-warning platform urgently produced during the Falklands War by gutting an HAS.2 and adding Thorn-EMI Searchwater surveillance radar with its antenna in a semi-retractable inflatable radome. The HAR.3 is an uprated SAR version used by the RAF, with MEL radar, Decca nav/doppler/computer and provision for a crew of four and six stretchers, 19 seated rescuees or a mix. The HAS.5 is an uprated ASW/SAR model, 30 of which were supplied to the Royal Navy. MEL Sea Searcher radar results in a bigger dorsal radome. Other changes include a new nav/attack system with precision positioning, passive sonobuoy equipment and advanced Lapads acoustic processing and display equipment. To make room, the cabin rear bulkhead was moved back 68in (1.72m). The latest RN version, to which almost all ASW survivors are being converted, is the HAS.6 with a completely new AQS-902G-DS digital system able to

process buoys and dipping sonar. Other improvements include upgraded ESM (electronic support measures), IFF, MAD and communications, and a sonar winch system increasing hover height to a maximum of 700ft (213m). Current export versions are of the Advanced Sea King family, with uprated gearbox and other parts, new rotors with composite blades (the tail rotor reverting to five blades) and other changes to reduce costs and enable weight to reach the figure given in the data.

In the early 1970s Westland developed the Commando as a dedicated land-based helicopter for tactical transport, casevac and logistic support. Features include a fuselage without a boat-type bottom, simple fixed landing gear and much role equipment. The Royal Navy Sea King HC.4 is a member of this family. Whereas the ASW versions have empty weights over 16,000lb (see data) the Commando, complete with crew, weighs about 12,390lb (5,620kg). Thus it can carry up to 45 troops, or a slung load of 8,000lb (3,628kg).

Below: The Federal German Marineflieger (naval air force) received twenty Sea King Mk 41 helicopters, operated in the SAR (search and rescue) role throughout Germany and the southern North Sea by Marineflieger Geschwader 5 (MFG 5) based at Nordholz. They have MEL dorsal radar and since delivery received new avionics.

Right: A large scanner (for the MEL Super Searcher radar) distinguishes the Royal Navy Sea King HAS.5, seen in this photograph with a full load of torpedoes as well as CAE Electronics MAD sensor and other stores. The box-like fairing on the nose is one of two forward-mounted Racal MIR-2 Orange Crop ESM passive receiver antennas.

Westland Lynx (Navy)

In the 1960s the famous names of the British helicopter industry had all been merged into Westland, while it was obvious a new helicopter was needed in the 8,000lb (3,629kg) class to replace the Scout, Wasp, Sycamore, Dragonfly and Whirlwind. In 1967 this need was addressed by the WG.13, a completely fresh design launched as the only British helicopter in a joint agreement with France. Five of the 13 prototypes were of a naval version. This featured the standard streamlined pod/boom fuselage, and advanced four-blade main rotor with probably the neatest hub yet seen (a shallow titanium forging holding the blades by flexible arms). The tailfin carries the rotor on the left and half tailplane on the right. The naval Lynx naturally incorporated totally different avionics and role equipment from army versions, but the most obvious difference was the landing gear. This comprises a fixed but steerable twin-wheel nose gear and fixed main gears with vertical shock struts designed for landing on pitching and rolling decks. Normally the main wheels are toed out at 27° for deck landing, and they have sprag (ratchet)

Origin: UK. Data for Lynx HAS.8.
Engines: Two 1,120shp Rolls-Royce Gem 42-1.
Dimensions: Diameter of main rotor 42ft 0in (12.8m); length overall (rotors turning) 50ft 0in (15.24m); length (folded) 35ft 7.2in (10.85m).
Weights: Empty 7,255lb (3,291kg); max loaded 11,300lb (5,125kg).
Performance: Max cruising speed 159mph (256km/h); range (as transport) 426 miles (685km); radius (ship attack, four Sea Skua) 170 miles (274km).
Armament: Two Sting Ray, Mk 44, Mk 46 or similar torpedoes, two Penguin or four Sea Skua or AS.12 anti-ship missiles, or two Mk 11 depth charges.
History: First flight (HAS.2 prototype) 25 May 1972, (HAS.8 tactical testbed) 25 January 1989.

brakes. Landing can be assisted by a hydraulic harpoon deck lock. After landing, the brakes are hydraulically released and the wheels rotated fore-and-aft for putting the machine in its hangar.

The initial version for the Royal Navy was the HAS.2, with the 900shp Gem 2 engine and Ferranti Seaspray radar in the nose. Westland delivered 60, plus 26 Mk 2(FN) to the French Aéronavale with French avionics. From the outset the Mk 2 could be used for ASW classification and strike, ASV search

and strike, SAR (search and rescue), reconnaissance, troop transport, fire support, communication and fleet liaison, and vertrep (vertical replenishment). Depending on how much ASW gear is installed the cabin can house ten troops or nine rescuees. In 1985-8, 54 HAS.2s were brought up to HAS.3 standard, with 1,120shp Gem 41-1 engines. All have MIR-2 ESM (electronic surveillance measures), dipping sonar linked with the AFCS (auto flight control system), and (progressively being added) ALQ-167 ECM jamming pods and Tracor M-130 chaff/flare dispensers. CAE internal MAD (magnetic-anomaly detector) internal receivers are being supplied. The Lynx Mk 4 is an equivalent French version.

The data refer to the next generation, the HAS.8, equivalent to the export Super Lynx. This has BERP composite blades, improved tail rotor control and a central tactical system which processes all inputs for a multifunction electronic display. The radar will be repackaged in the chin position, leaving the nose for a GEC Sea Owl thermal imager. South Korea has ordered 12, with Sea Skua missiles.

Above: When operating in the anti-ship role the Royal Navy Lynx HAS.2 carries four Sea Skua missiles.

Below: Side profile of a standard Lynx HAS.2 of the Royal Navy. The HAS.3 is virtually identical and the HAS.8 differs in having been fitted with a reverse-direction tail rotor.

ROYAL NAVY   ZD263   DANCER→   PO

Westland Lynx (Army)

Origin: UK. Data for AH.1.
Engines: Two 900shp Rolls-Royce Gem 2.
Dimensions: Diameter of main rotor 42ft 0in (12.8m); length overall (rotors turning) 49ft 9in (15.163m).
Weights: Empty 5,683lb (2,578kg); max loaded 10,000lb (4,536kg).
Performance: Max cruising speed 161mph (259km/h); hovering ceiling out of ground effect 10,600ft (3,230m); typical range as troop transport, with reserves 336 miles (540km).
Armament: Eight TOW, HOT, Hellfire or similar anti-armour missiles, as well as two 20mm cannon firing ahead or a pintle-mounted 7.62mm machine gun in the cabin. Wide range of other guns, rocket pods, minelaying gear and other weapons.
History: First flight 21 March 1971, (production AH.5) 23 February 1985, (AH.7) 7 November 1985, (AH.9) 1990.

As explained in the preceding entry, the Lynx was developed to undertake an exceptional range of army and navy missions. Originally the Army version was a simple utility machine, and all five of the original batch of prototypes were to this configuration. Apart from the completely new and rather complex three-shaft engine, one of the few really advanced features was the gearbox, with W-N conformal gearteeth, which enabled the design to be very compact. Together with the outstanding rotor hub, this gave the helicopter a low profile, despite the fact that the cabin internal height is 7in (178mm) greater than that of a UH-1. Early flight trials confirmed that the Lynx has outstanding agility, with the power to perform repeated rolls or loops, or any other manoeuvres. As for performance, the company demonstrator, refitted with BERP III rotor blades and other modifications, but with normal Mk 41-1 engines, currently holds the world helicopter speed record at 249.09mph (400.87km/h).

Westland delivered 113 of the original AH.1 version, of which (despite the Falklands War, in which they were very valuable) 108 remained in use in 1989. Powered by 900shp Mk 2 engines, the AH.1 had simple skid gear, but comprehensive avionics for night and adverse weather missions, including an automatic flight-control system, VOR/ILS, doppler, Tacan and three-axis autostabilization. Seats are pro-

vided for the pilot and co-pilot or observer and up to 10 armed troops as an alternative to missile teams or cargo. From 1981 a total of 60 AH.1s were equipped to fire TOW missiles, with British Aerospace roof sights which are being upgraded by the addition of a GEC far-IR thermal imager for use at night or in poor visibility. Other upgrades include the Sanders ALQ-144 active IR jammer, installed under the tailboom, and the Ferranti AWARE-3 radar warning receiver. Other role equipment can include a pintle mount for a side gun, vertical and/or oblique cameras, night flares, low-light TV, IR linescan, searchlight, clip-on rescue hoist, waterproof floor and specialized communications.

In 1984 flight testing began of two trials aircraft to prove

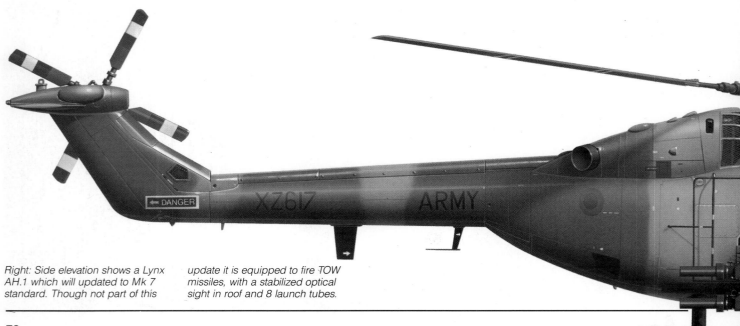

Right: Side elevation shows a Lynx AH.1 which will updated to Mk 7 standard. Though not part of this update it is equipped to fire TOW missiles, with a stabilized optical sight in roof and 8 launch tubes.